Mindfulness Techniques

Simple Mindfulness Steps on How to Suffer Less
When Suffering is Inevitable

(How to Find Peace and Cure Anxiety and Stress)

Joshua Hill

Published by Rob Miles

© **Joshua Hill**

All Rights Reserved

Mindfulness Techniques: Simple Mindfulness Steps on How to Suffer Less When Suffering is Inevitable (How to Find Peace and Cure Anxiety and Stress)

ISBN 978-1-989990-93-3

All rights reserved. No part of this guide may be reproduced in any form without permission in writing from the publisher except in the case of brief quotations embodied in critical articles or reviews.

LEGAL & DISCLAIMER

The information contained in this book is not designed to replace or take the place of any form of medicine or professional medical advice. The information in this book has been provided for educational and entertainment purposes only.

The information contained in this book has been compiled from sources deemed reliable, and it is accurate to the best of the Author's knowledge; however, the Author cannot guarantee its accuracy and validity and cannot be held liable for any errors or omissions. Changes are periodically made to this book. You must consult your doctor or get professional medical advice before using any of the suggested remedies, techniques, or information in this book.

Upon using the information contained in this book, you agree to hold harmless the Author from and against any damages, costs, and expenses, including any legal fees potentially resulting from the application of any of the information provided by this guide. This disclaimer applies to any damages or injury caused by the use and application, whether directly or indirectly, of any advice or information presented, whether for breach of contract, tort, negligence, personal injury, criminal intent, or under any other cause of action.

You agree to accept all risks of using the information presented inside this book. You need to consult a professional medical practitioner in order to ensure you are both able and healthy enough to participate in this program.

Table of Contents

INTRODUCTION 1

CHAPTER 1: EXPLAINING MINDFULNESS 8

CHAPTER 2: THE SAFE PLACE MEDITATION 15

CHAPTER 3: MINDFULNESS VERSUS MEDITATION 34

CHAPTER 4: MEDITATION AND NEGATIVE EMOTIONS 39

CHAPTER 5: UNDERSTANDING WHAT IT MEANS TO FOCUS 45

CHAPTER 6: THE MARKS OF EXISTENCE 50

CHAPTER 7: MINDFUL SELF-TRANSFORMATION 62

CHAPTER 8: ACTIVE LISTENING 73

CHAPTER 9: MANAGING ANGER WITH MINDFULNESS 78

CHAPTER 10: RAIN – A FOUR-STEP PROCESS FOR USING MINDFULNESS IN DIFFICULT SITUATIONS 84

CHAPTER 11: BODY SCAN TECHNIQUE 90

CHAPTER 12: RELIEVE STRESS, SELF – IMPROVEMENT AND SELF-CONTROL WITH MEDITATION 93

CHAPTER 13: TIPS FOR PRACTICING THE MEDITATION 97

CHAPTER 14: MINDFUL MEDITATION 108

CHAPTER 15: THE HEART OF THE ROSE MEDITATION TECHNIQUE 121

CHAPTER 16: NEURAL PATHWAYS 124

CHAPTER 17: MINDFUL OBSERVATION............................ 135

CHAPTER 18: UNDERSTANDING FEAR AND ANXIETY 146

CHAPTER 19: REDUCING STRESS AND ANXIETY 154

CHAPTER 20: EXERCISE YOUR STRESS AWAY 172

CONCLUSION.. 183

Introduction

Every day, more and more people are finding their way because they are learning how to make mindful meditation into a habit they are able to embrace on a daily basis. The mind works in an extraordinary manner and is capable of looking inward as well as looking in an outward direction. Quite often, the noise of the world around us confuses us and we start to think outside of this moment in time, thus losing the opportunity of enjoying the moment before it has gone forever. You see, that's the basis for mindfulness. It is simply making the most of your life by being present in it. How could you not be present? Think about it for a moment. How many hours a day do you think about things that have happened in the past, even if they were only a few hours ago? How many times do you look forward in your life and worry about things that have not yet happened?

Mindfulness helps you to overcome this and mindfulness meditation helps to give you clarity which is something people are seeking in their lives these days, but which they seek in all the wrong places.

You need to go back in time to understand the significance of Mindfulness Meditation and this book will take you there, because I believe that you do need to know about the roots of the practice so that you have a more sustained knowledge of why you are meditating and the overall effects of that meditation. This book is aimed at beginners and people who have already started to meditate, because getting the message across in a way that persuades is not always achieved by technical books or lessons with teachers who are not that mindful themselves! In fact, I have to admit that students I have had the pleasure to teach have recounted all kinds of horrors in their search for inner peace, when the answers to their queries are always so straightforward and simple.

The largest problem was the concept of meditation. This is taught in various ways and some of these actually put concentration as a priority when, in fact, the mind is letting go rather than consciously thinking about the process of letting go. While you attempt to let go, you can never actually do it, because your mind is too occupied trying to do it. That's why this book has been written. I wanted students to have one place of reference where all the information that they obtain is adequate and explains things in full. You will learn much from reading the rest of this book and this could be life-changing. All I would ask is that you give yourself to the process and decide to start when you feel that you are ready. There are also exercises leading up to meditation so that you can step out of the busy world that you are accustomed to, and gradually move toward achieving the inner peace that everyone deserves, but that not all obtain.

Meditation is useful for many purposes including the relief of anxiety, depression, stress, pain and illness, but more than that it will lead you to a place of happiness within yourself so that all of the agonies of the world can be dealt with in a better way. When you have the inner strength that mindfulness meditation gives you, you are stronger, happier and more complete as a human being.

The book will show you from very basic instructions in a step by step manner how to meditate, and what to expect when you do meditate. It shows you how to overcome the barriers that everyone faces when they first attempt to meditate but it does more than that. It also gives you alternative ways to meditate and to use meditation in your day to day lives so that it helps you to find the peace that you have been looking for. There isn't just one way to meditate. Mindfulness practiced in everyday life can help you to get a better understanding of meditation and become a part of the meditation process. In fact, I have written about the use of mantras, the use of chanting, the use of guided meditation and the use of inspiration to help you through the process of learning, so that you can make the most of the whole experience.

There is so much more to life than the stresses and strains that you may have become accustomed to. In this world, we put our priorities in the wrong things and it is our expectations that make us disappointed in the world. However, mindfulness brings you back to basics so that you don't have the same expectations either of others or of yourself. Judgement is not part of the picture. You may say that's not possible, but it is not only possible, but could prove to be a turning point in your life. In preparation for meditation, I have pointed out what's necessary and what's not. There are so many misconceptions about meditation that the book has attempted to demystify the process so that you can approach your meditation experience with realistic expectations and without letting your own code of judgment get in the way of your process.

Although Buddhism and other religions are mentioned, you do not need to be affiliated to any religion to benefit from meditation. It is independent of those religions although does follow the philosophy of Buddhism because it's a common sense approach to life that will improve your life. Go into it with an open mind. If you find that you are unable to relax, you will find the exercises given in the book will help you to relax. It is a wise move to try these before you try meditation. There are also mindfulness exercises that you can introduce into your life to make the tasks that you are faced with in your day to day life less onerous. Life doesn't have to be harsh and just because it presents tasks that you don't much like doing, it doesn't mean that you cannot approach those jobs at the right time and in the right frame of mind to make them easier and less stressful.

Mindfulness is all about being in the moment, as you will learn throughout the book.

I hope that you are approaching the book with an open mind and that you are ready to improve your life, because that's the purpose of writing it; to help you to live your life to its fullest advantage, taking in the happiness and the positivity that life offers you without allowing negativity to get in the way. Meditation will help you to do just that, but it also helps you in so many other ways as you will find out when you read the chapter showing the benefits of meditation. The benefits are an ongoing process as you will see from the scientific viewpoint contained within the book. The whole point is to learn as much as you can about why mindfulness meditation helps you, so that you are not easily deterred from the new route that your life is about to take.

Chapter 1: Explaining Mindfulness

I could organize this book in such a manner that you will need to build up to mindfulness. I could discuss how horrible for you stress is, or I could discuss neuroscience.

But I'll come to that later. What you most likely wish to know right off the bat is simply what mindfulness is. Where did it originate from? And how can you utilize it just to get a little calmer and comfortable in your life?

We'll take a look at that initially and from there, we'll look into how you can use some more technical neuroscience so as to delve into the more extensive capabilities of your brain.

So what precisely is mindfulness? Basically, mindfulness is a kind of meditation that has been embraced by CBT. CBT, consequently, is 'cognitive behavioral therapy'; a psychotherapeutic process that can be utilized to address all manner of psychological problems such as anxiety, fears, addiction, etc.

Mindfulness basically provides us a tool that we can utilize to not only soothe our thoughts and get away from the stressors of the day but also review the contents of our mind with the goal of self-improvement.

Meditation typically has something of a 'bad' image. That is to say that a bunch of people connect it with religion or esoteric concepts and they believe that they simply cannot meditate unless they're' spiritual'. This could be off-putting for somebody who doesn't keep any religious ideas or who doesn't like mystical concepts as a whole.

But as a matter of fact, you can engage in meditation no matter if you are religious or an atheist. All meditation truly is, is a guided effort to regulate your thoughts and the content of your mind and thus to gain some calmness and quiet or at minimum to be ready to comprehend the contents of your own brain better.

Often this implies entirely muting all thoughts. Many kinds of meditation, like transcendental meditation, advise you to think of 'completely nothing' and frequently this is accomplished by concentrating on your breathing, a mantra or a physical item such as a candle flame. This can be tough for novices, as they regularly find their mind straying.

The strategy behind mindfulness meditation then is not to attempt and unload your thoughts but rather to just step back from them and 'monitor' them like a separated third party. By doing this, you aren't allowing your thoughts influence you and make you worried but you likewise aren't going to deal with not being 'permitted' to think anything.

At the same time, utilizing this technique will also enable you to end up being more aware of your own feelings and thus able to modify any thoughts that are leading you into problems. For example, if you regularly find yourself considering the ways that you might harm yourself, you might observe that this is a bad habit and after that try to mend that.

This may be the long-term objective of mindfulness when utilized in CBT. In the short-term, however, we are merely to use it so as to extract ourselves from our feelings and emotions to ensure that we can get some tranquility and therefore recover ready to take on the day ahead.

Mindfulness in Daily Life

This is what mindfulness describes in many cases but it has likewise been appropriated to suggest a lot more. If mindfulness means being more familiar with your thoughts, then it can likewise be used outside of meditation and to the way you deal with your day. In this instance, mindfulness merely means being conscious of what you're concentrating on and what you're feeling at any given point. This works due to the fact that very frequently you'll find that your mind isn't possibly where it ought to be.

For instance, if you are going through a lovely scenic woodland but you are thinking of work, then as far as your body is involved, you may as well be at your job. In this situation, mindfulness can be utilized just to make yourself more knowledgeable about where you are and to, in fact, pay attention to what's around you. That implies feeling the wind on your skin, checking out the lovely flowers and smelling the clean air. When you perform all that, you will gain a lot more from the experience.

Also, you can use mindfulness to guide your awareness to all manner of other things. For instance, your physical sensations. Often we aren't familiar with simply how we're sitting or how we're standing.

Take a minute now to reflect on this. How relaxed are you at the minute? Does any area of your body hurt? In case you're sitting, then where is the majority of pressure on you? Can you sense your clothes against your body? A watch, perhaps? How cozy are you?

This sort of mindfulness can be beneficial if you wish to attempt and remedy your posture but also if you wish to enhance your capabilities in sports or just to obtain more success.

Being more mindful of the way you talk can at the same time help you to speak more smoothly, to stop using demeaning words, to stop cussing, or to alter the entire way that people view you. For instance, if you wish to sound more educated, then you can just try utilizing bigger words or talking a tad more slowly.

You can also utilize mindfulness to be more satisfied in day-to-day life. Just try to stop allowing negative feelings to impact you by identifying them as momentary and troublesome. You can just 'observe' that you're getting angry and recognize that your feelings will be polluted by that. With practice, this can make you a much more relaxed and much healthier individual.

But what do you discover when you make an effort and do this? In all probability, you'll discover that you forget. This is just the same way that you fail to remember to get bread whenever your partner asks you to. And it's just the same way you fail to remember to grab your keys while exiting the house.

The point is, the majority of the time we have no authority over what we're concentrated on or what we're focusing on. And because of this, we find ourselves overlooking things, embracing bad habits or worrying when we ought to be enjoying ourselves.

Practicing mindfulness both as a type of meditation and throughout the day can, as a result, help you to enhance your ability to regulate your thoughts and therefore to choose how you want to strengthen yourself and what you wish to focus on.

Chapter 2: The Safe Place Meditation

This meditation is perfect for defeating anxiety and for getting in a quieter and more convenient space of mind.

It originates from the ancient Eastern culture and it was used by monks during their initiation period, where they had to face extremely hard circumstances. Nowadays, it is often practised by endurance athletes, that experience prolonged pain and suffering during training and races.

Courtney Dauwalter, a famous ultrarunner and winner of the 2018 edition ofMoab 240, a 240 miles running race, reported multiple times how she used this technique to go through the most difficult moments of the event.

To give you a quick insight on what we are going to do during the meditation, here is a small recap of the main steps of the practice. After focusing on ourselves and entering a profound space of relaxation, we will picture in our mind a place that reminds us of a beautiful and peaceful moment we have experienced in the past. Than, we will imagine ourselves inside the image and rest our awareness in this quiet space.

That is everything there is to know to approach the practice with enough background information to get the most out of it.

So, let's get started!

Find a comfortable, relaxed and balanced position. Give yourself permission to be completely present for yourself, and let your body and mind calm down until they become soft and relaxed.

Breathe in, feel relaxed...

breathe out, feel calm...

Breathe in, feel relaxed...

breathe out, feel calm...

Breathe in, feel relaxed...

breathe out, feel calm…

Breathe in, feel relaxed…

breathe out, feel calm…

Allow the mind to distance itself from all thoughts and orientate awareness on your breath. Breathe naturally and do not force a specific rhythm. Let your breath come and go.

Carefully, now, drive your attention from the breath to the space in which you are.

Feel the energy and atmosphere of this space as it permeates all of your being. Notice the noises in the background. Maybe there is a clock ticking, maybe there are cars passing just outside your windows. Whatever you feel it is fine, let your attention rest on the external.

Breathe in, feel relaxed…

breathe out, feel calm…

Breathe in, feel relaxed…

breathe out, feel calm…

Breathe in, feel relaxed…

breathe out, feel calm...

Breathe in, feel relaxed...

breathe out, feel calm...

Now bring the attention back to the breath. Take your time and you will naturally reach a place of warmth and ease.

There is nothing to do here, nothing to think or to worry about. Just rest your attention on the breath, following each inhalation and exhalation with curiosity, falling into the rhythm of your very own body.

If you want, you can place your hands on your belly. This will help you enter in connection with the natural movement of the air entering through your nose and exciting trough the mouth.

Breathe in, feel relaxed...

breathe out, feel calm...

Breathe in, feel relaxed...

breathe out, feel calm...

Breathe in, feel relaxed...

breathe out, feel calm...

Breathe in, feel relaxed...

breathe out, feel calm...

Breathe in, feel relaxed...

breathe out, feel calm...

Breathe in, feel relaxed...

breathe out, feel calm...

Breathe in, feel relaxed...

breathe out, feel calm...

Breathe in, feel relaxed...

breathe out, feel calm...

I will give you a few more minutes to get into this zone, as we will than begin the actual practice.

Breathe in, feel relaxed...

breathe out, feel calm...

Breathe in, feel relaxed...

breathe out, feel calm...

Breathe in, feel relaxed...

breathe out, feel calm...

Breathe in, feel relaxed...

breathe out, feel calm...

Breathe in, feel relaxed...

breathe out, feel calm...

Breathe in, feel relaxed...

breathe out, feel calm...

Breathe in, feel relaxed...

breathe out, feel calm...

Breathe in, feel relaxed...

breathe out, feel calm...

Breathe in, feel relaxed...

breathe out, feel calm...

Breathe in, feel relaxed...

breathe out, feel calm...

Breathe in, feel relaxed...

breathe out, feel calm...

Breathe in, feel relaxed...

breathe out, feel calm...

Breathe in, feel relaxed...

breathe out, feel calm...

Breathe in, feel relaxed...

breathe out, feel calm...

Breathe in, feel relaxed...

breathe out, feel calm...

Breathe in, feel relaxed...

breathe out, feel calm...

Now start thinking about a moment in the past where you felt incredibly good and safe. Do not rush the process, let the memory come to your mind in a natural way. This is extremely important, because remember: in meditation there is nothing to do, everything comes naturally and arises from within.

Breathe in, feel relaxed...

breathe out, feel calm...

Breathe in, feel relaxed...

breathe out, feel calm...

Breathe in, feel relaxed...

breathe out, feel calm...

Breathe in, feel relaxed...

breathe out, feel calm...

If the memory has come to your mind, ask yourself how the location was. Was it in nature? Maybe at home? Just think about it and picture it inside your mind.

Breathe in, feel relaxed...

breathe out, feel calm...

Breathe in, feel relaxed...

breathe out, feel calm...

Breathe in, feel relaxed...

breathe out, feel calm...

Breathe in, feel relaxed...

breathe out, feel calm...

After you have got the general idea, try to go a bit deeper and picture a bit more details of the scene. Figure out the sounds, the smells and the feelings that the place is providing for you. There is no right or wrong way to do this, just try to get as much details as possible, really painting a beautiful and complete picture of the place inside your mind.

Breathe in, feel relaxed...

breathe out, feel calm...

Breathe in, feel relaxed...

breathe out, feel calm...

Breathe in, feel relaxed...

breathe out, feel calm...

Breathe in, feel relaxed...

breathe out, feel calm...

Breathe in, feel relaxed...

breathe out, feel calm...

Breathe in, feel relaxed...

breathe out, feel calm...

Breathe in, feel relaxed...

breathe out, feel calm...

Breathe in, feel relaxed...

breathe out, feel calm...

Focus on the light and the background noise, as getting in touch with the smaller details can help a lot in crafting a complete image.

Breathe in, feel relaxed...

breathe out, feel calm...

Breathe in, feel relaxed...

breathe out, feel calm...

Breathe in, feel relaxed...

breathe out, feel calm...

Breathe in, feel relaxed...

breathe out, feel calm...

Breathe in, feel relaxed...

breathe out, feel calm...

Breathe in, feel relaxed...

breathe out, feel calm...

Breathe in, feel relaxed...

breathe out, feel calm...

Breathe in, feel relaxed...

breathe out, feel calm...

Now that you have the picture clear in your head, it is time to start living in this safe place. Enter the picture with your mind and imagine as if you were there for real. The mind cannot tell the difference between a "fake" or "real" experience, so it does not matter that you are not there physically. If you can imagine to be there, you are actually there.

I know that this is going on a bit of a philosophical path, but you will get a full understanding once you have experienced the entire practice.

Breathe in, feel relaxed...

breathe out, feel calm...

Breathe in, feel relaxed...

breathe out, feel calm...

Breathe in, feel relaxed...

breathe out, feel calm...

Breathe in, feel relaxed...

breathe out, feel calm...

Breathe in, feel relaxed...

breathe out, feel calm...

Breathe in, feel relaxed...

breathe out, feel calm...

Breathe in, feel relaxed...

breathe out, feel calm...

Breathe in, feel relaxed...

breathe out, feel calm...

With every breath, try to get a little deeper and feel a little more inside your safe space. This is a space that is completely yours and that does not hold any judgement at all. You can do whatever you want here, as there are no physical limits, no laws, no rules to follow. In this safe space, reality bends under your control and you are the master of everything, while still being a visitor of the space.

Breathe in, feel relaxed...

breathe out, feel calm...

Breathe in, feel relaxed...

breathe out, feel calm...

Breathe in, feel relaxed...

breathe out, feel calm...

Breathe in, feel relaxed...

breathe out, feel calm...

Breathe in, feel relaxed...

breathe out, feel calm...

Breathe in, feel relaxed...

breathe out, feel calm...

Breathe in, feel relaxed...

breathe out, feel calm...

Breathe in, feel relaxed...

breathe out, feel calm...

I will give you a few minutes to experience the safety of this space by yourself. Let your mind free, as it has nothing to worry about.

Breathe in, feel relaxed...

breathe out, feel calm...

Breathe in, feel relaxed...

breathe out, feel calm...

Breathe in, feel relaxed...

breathe out, feel calm...

Breathe in, feel relaxed...

breathe out, feel calm...

Breathe in, feel relaxed...

breathe out, feel calm...

Breathe in, feel relaxed...

breathe out, feel calm...

Breathe in, feel relaxed...

breathe out, feel calm...

Breathe in, feel relaxed...

breathe out, feel calm...

Breathe in, feel relaxed...

breathe out, feel calm...

Breathe in, feel relaxed...

breathe out, feel calm...

Breathe in, feel relaxed...

breathe out, feel calm...

Breathe in, feel relaxed...

breathe out, feel calm...

Breathe in, feel relaxed...

breathe out, feel calm...

Breathe in, feel relaxed...

breathe out, feel calm...

Breathe in, feel relaxed...

breathe out, feel calm...

Breathe in, feel relaxed...

breathe out, feel calm...

Breathe in, feel relaxed...

breathe out, feel calm...

Breathe in, feel relaxed...

breathe out, feel calm...

Breathe in, feel relaxed...

breathe out, feel calm...

Breathe in, feel relaxed...

breathe out, feel calm...

Breathe in, feel relaxed...

breathe out, feel calm...

Breathe in, feel relaxed...

breathe out, feel calm...

Breathe in, feel relaxed...

breathe out, feel calm...

And now that we are approaching the end of the practice, just know that you can enter this space whenever you desire. It will always be there for you, it will not go away. Once you discover this state of mind, or space, inside of you, you know that every time you feel anxious or worried, you can go back to this sensation and melt everything away.

Feel the freedom, as freedom is the cure.

Breathe in, feel relaxed...

breathe out, feel calm...

Breathe in, feel relaxed...

breathe out, feel calm...

Breathe in, feel relaxed...

breathe out, feel calm...

Breathe in, feel relaxed...

breathe out, feel calm...

Breathe in, feel relaxed...

breathe out, feel calm...

Breathe in, feel relaxed...

breathe out, feel calm...

Breathe in, feel relaxed...

breathe out, feel calm...

Breathe in, feel relaxed...

breathe out, feel calm...

Now bring the attention back to the body and start feeling your arms and legs once again. You can close your hands or move your fingers, just to take control of the space around you.

Please, keep the eyes closed for now and enjoy the beautiful moment you are living. You have given yourself the time to feel better and that is absolutely incredible.

Breathe in, feel relaxed...

breathe out, feel calm...

Breathe in, feel relaxed...

breathe out, feel calm...

Breathe in, feel relaxed...

breathe out, feel calm...

Breathe in, feel relaxed...

breathe out, feel calm...

Now become aware of the environment around you once again. Feel the different sounds, the temperature of the room you are in and once you are ready, open the eyes again.

Chapter 3: Mindfulness Versus Meditation

As I've mentioned previously, mindfulness is in vogue currently that people keep saying the term over and over again. In fact, it has been repeated so much and so frequently that it almost means nothing. Not surprisingly, people confuse it with meditation. Indeed, if you do a simple search for meditation and mindfulness, it would seem that most people use them interchangeably. It's easy to see why. They do have a lot in common.

When people engage in meditation practice, one of their objectives is to decrease stress. They want to be more at peace. Sounds familiar, right? That's exactly the kind of goals many people who try mindfulness are shooting for. But there's actually quite a bit of difference between mindfulness and meditation.

The shell versus the house

With mindfulness, you're essentially just dealing with a tiny segment of the many different parts that make up meditation. With mindfulness, you're just looking to be aware of a particular point in time. You're just trying to live in the moment. With meditation, on the other hand, you are looking to change your consciousness. You're looking to change your perspective.

While living in the present moment is one key part of that, it can definitely go much deeper. It can be quite extensive and its reach can go far and wide indeed as far as your personal life is concerned.

Mindfulness is kind of like a capsule portion of what you can possibly achieve with your meditative practice. This leads of course to different objectives.

Different objectives

The main objective of mindfulness is to simply calm down, feel less stressed, and achieve a higher level of control over your daily waking life.

In the big scheme of things, this set of objectives is actually quite narrow, at least when compared to the objectives people often have with meditation. Because meditation practice is not just about achieving inner peace and inner calm, it can be a gateway to higher states of spiritual consciousness.

Now, I know in our secular American society, people are scared about spirituality and religion. But even if you do not believe in religion, there is still a strong spiritual component present in the human experience. You would really be doing yourself a big disservice to completely ignore the spiritual part of your psyche.

Even if your objectives are completely secular and practical, working with your spiritual side can help you get your desired outcomes sooner rather than later.

Relaxation versus altered higher states of consciousness

Meditation uses the same gateway as mindfulness, let's get that out of the way. Both have to go through the same door. This door of course is relaxation.

However, they differ greatly because with mindfulness you stop at the door. Once you reach the relaxation stage, you're done. With meditation, you just treat it as a door because your whole point is to get past the door. Your whole point is to keep going and either keep digging deeper or reaching higher.

Focus versus consciousness

Meditation is all about achieving a higher degree of consciousness. Again, this doesn't have to be necessarily spiritual or mystical, but it is definitely necessary for a more purposeful life and more powerful life. This level of consciousness that you're getting can fit and flow into other areas of your life.

Mindfulness, on the other hand, is more tightly contained to focusing. All the mindfulness techniques that I will outline here involve focus. It stops at the power of focus. Of course, if you're doing meditation, focus is just one part of the equation. Once you tap into focus, it then triggers other things you could be doing which lead to different outcomes.

The bottom line

The bottom line with mindfulness is quite simple. It's all about mental alertness, being awake on a moment-by-moment basis. That's all it is. It's not about gaining insights. It's not about profoundly changing the way you think so certain issues from your past no longer haunt you. It's not about that if you don't want it to be so.

By simply choosing to be mentally alert and awake on a moment-by-moment basis, you can say goodbye to a lot of your daily stresses, pressures, and other elements in your life that tend to grind you down.

Chapter 4: Meditation And Negative Emotions

When you relax and focus on your inner peace, you can improve your mental health. In research that was later published in the JAMA Internal Medicine in 2014, researchers found that meditation programs helped reduce the symptoms of anxiety and depression. Another scientific study published in 2018 in the Psychiatric Review, found out that subjects that suffered from generalized anxiety enjoyed a better reduction in stressful symptoms. Let us look at the various ways that meditation can help in handling mental issues.

Meditation has the capability to handle negative emotions in a way that is healthy and effective. You need to remember that emotions are the core of your actions. Your whole human experience is enshrined in emotions, right from your childhood. You have experienced waves of happiness, sadness, anger, and more.

When you meditate, you learn how to identify emotions deep within yourself so that you can study them, learn more about them, and then release them. The various ancient traditions of the east, such as Daoism, Buddhism, and Hinduism, have long studies man's emotions, and they do this with the aim of going past human suffering. They have devoted hundreds of revelations, experiments, and insight to discover the emotions that are ideal to the human race.

The Process: Seeing Clearly

Here, you have to look at the emotion in a different way. First, you have to recognize the emotion that you have encountered, then label the emotion before you can go ahead to handle it. The negative emotion can be fear, sadness, or anything else. Before you can handle it, go ahead and identify it/ When you identify the emotion, you will handle it much easier.

When you label the emotion, don't own it; instead, use words that will make the emotion look much better and easier to handle.

After you label the emotion, the next thing is you have to take a few breaths and then divert your attention from the emotion. This means you don't pay any attention to the root cause of the emotion; rather, you need to look at the attention itself. You accept that the feeling is there, but you don't put your emotion on it.

Examine

After you put a name to the emotion, the next thing is to try and know what caused it. Look at the issues that trigger the feeling at any moment, and then note them down if possible. You don't need to look at the root causes right from childhood but know what is happening right here. Once you look at the various causes of the emotion, try and identify them, and handle them. The next thing is to try and look at what the effects of the emotions are in your body. What do you feel when the emotion happens? Where does the feeling take you, and how does it feel? What do you think about the feeling?

Next, look deep into yourself and understand what the feeling is all about. Can you put a size to the feeling? The color and consistency? If the emotion wasn't there at the moment, where did it come from? Learn as much as you can about the emotion. Remember that emotions make the bulk of our lives and you need to know so much about it so that you aren't a slave to it.

Release

You need to leave whatever it is that is affecting you but don't talk about it even with your friends. Just let it off in the best way ever. The outcome of the process is in various ways. First, you will be clear with the emotion; you will be composed when you have the emotion in check, and you know what it is. You also get to know the emotion what triggers it and the effects it has on your life. The final benefit is to liberate yourself from the emotion.

Many times, you can find out that the emotion points to something which needs attention from you in your life. This will prompt you to take action. External actions are all about making sure you handle what causes the issue externally. When you go through the emotions, you will find that the negative emotion disappears into thin air. It might also lose its power over you, or it can transform into a totally different thing. Here are other steps that you can take up to make your life better using meditation.

Acknowledge the Temporary Nature of the Emotion

When you have a negative emotion burdening you, the next thing is that you need to know that the emotions which you experience are not permanent. The negative emotions will come up, be around for a while then disappear. They are like waves of the sea they come and go. Your role in this sense is just to be a witness to the wave of the emotion. You observe it as it changes its form and then disappears eventually. Many people take the emotions very seriously and personally, which shouldn't be the case. When you use mindfulness, you will be able to view the emotion as a series of mental events that pass through in a temporary manner.

Trust Yourself

When you have the emotion in check, the next step would be to trust your decisions. The aim is to identify the emotion then come up with various decisions that can allow you to handle the issue. These decisions need to be ideal for your situation.

Chapter 5: Understanding What It Means To Focus

So what exactly is the focus? What does focusing means to you? Having a good sense of focus and concentration is something that needs to be trained deliberately to a certain degree depending on the nature of your being. Some people are naturally good "focusers", usually equipped with an innate ability to do something for hours and hours if they found something they really liked, or loved to do.

They would just pour all their attention on it to feel good and milk the pleasure of doing it over and over again without feeling like a chore that needs to be completed. A child who loves his toy Legos, would spend all his time trying to build something out of his imagination and would just sit there and play with it all day long. One who fell in love with a picture book would read it over and over again every night, before she goes to bed.

It is the same thing and privilege that applies to an adult to have the opportunity to choose what she puts her attention on too. But as we grew out of our small bodies and our minds have expanded with new knowledge and information we have picked up along our trail, we start to lose interests in many simple things we once loved so much, when the routes around us get paved wider, exposing us to limitless options and choices.

You get caught up with the latest trends and fads and spend hours and hours on the internet prowling through social media sites, scrutinizing lives of people you don't even know personally. You start stirring up thought-provoking feelings (towards the negative direction) and emotions of discomfort with new findings and observations, judgments of others naturally start to build over time as you begin to compare your own life to them and that is the start of a very toxic relation-ship between you and your mind.

Introducing and practicing mindfulness in a modern lifestyle has proved to be nearly one of the biggest challenge in this advanced digital world we are living in right now. It has robbed us of many simple pleasures in life that we would have enjoyed otherwise if we weren't spending all of our free time on the screen of some sort to engage in activities that might not be serving us well. In this day and time, focusing on one task at a time is something that very little people do.

Most people can hardly get through a meal without meddling with a mobile device, tapping the screen while having the other hand armed with a fork or spoon but eyes still glued to the glaring small screen. It isn't so bad if there wasn't someone else sitting across you on the table, but that isn't even the worst-case scenario. Sometimes, even a table of 4 or a bigger group of people would just all be on their own devices in their own little world around the same table.

It is no rocket science that distances, connections, and bonds truly can't be measured by the tangible number of steps you are away from that living breathing person. You can be right on their heels and under their noses and still feel like they are a million miles away. Choosing what you want to focus on is something that needs attention and practice. Do you choose to connect with your loved ones and get through a meal properly or do you choose to interact with virtual beings on your screen?

We all have a choice. We always do. You pick for yourself every single time. If your intention is to spend time with that person, whether it is a friend, a partner, or your family member, give them the credit and attention that they are worth that much more. If not, don't waste your time trying to schedule a date to get together if no one is going to be present in that moment to connect with each other.

Where you put your focus and attention on, it gets bigger. If it is connection and love you crave and desire for in your life, you have to do the groundwork to direct it there intentionally in order to get back what "you deserve".

You have to make the effort to shift your focus and concentration to the right places and where you want it to grow. That is focus well spent and well done. Because focus equates to time, effort and even money sometimes. Make sure you use it wisely and distribute it to places and people who will help you elevate your senses, bring joy and peace into your life.

Chapter 6: The Marks Of Existence

In Buddhism, there are three marks of existence that describe the characteristics of everything within' the physical world, including mental activity and psychological experience. Most can agree that these three marks truly exist and that they can be found in virtually everything on the physical plane of existence. These three characteristics include impermanence, suffering, and egolessness or non-self. When you thoroughly examine and become aware of these marks, you will have an easier time abandoning the grasping and clinging tendencies that bind us together.

Impermanence (Anicca)

The idea of impermanence is that it is the fundamental property of everything that is conditioned. That means that everything that is conditioned is impermanent and that it is in a constant state of flux. Knowing this, everything that is in a state of flux and that is impermanent has the ability to be liberated.

Throughout our entire life, things, emotional states we attach ourselves to and ideas. Whenever

something changes, dies, or cannot be replicated, we enter states of anger, envy, and sadness. Because of our tendency to see ourselves as permanent things and to see other things and people as permanent things as well, we tend to cling to them deeply. While we deeply cling to them, we fail to realize the deeper understanding that all things, even ourselves, are impermanent. They do not exist forever and therefore they cannot possibly exist within' our lives forever.

When you abandon the idea that you are permanent, you give yourself the chance to be liberated from the clinging that you experience with things that you desire, as well as the negative effects that arise when those things change around you. As a result, you give yourself the ability to release your fears, disappointments, and regrets that you experience when these natural and inevitable changes take place. You give yourself the ability to be liberated from these feelings and experiences and give yourself the chance to be as enlightened as you possibly can be.

When you are able to nourish your insight into impermanence on a daily basis, you have the ability to live a deeper existence, experience less suffering, and gain more enjoyment out of life. When you are able to live in the moment and appreciate all that is occurring around you here and now, you are able to experience deeper gratitude for it and thus will end up feeling more peaceful and oftentimes happier as well. From this state, when you encounter experiences where you feel pain and suffering, you know that it is impermanent and that it too shall pass.

The lesson of impermanence is something that is not regarded often in today's society. We have a tendency to cling desperately to the things that we desire and greatly fear any changes that take place around us. Yet, things are changing around us possibly faster than ever before. It may even be the rapid speed of change that further encourages our need to cling harder to the things we care so deeply about. If you think about it, though, this gives even more reason as to why you should be learning about the teachings of impermanence.

These days, material goods are a major part of society. We all have vast amounts of material possessions, whether we are considered wealthy or poor. You may look around you right now and realize the number of objects that lie around you. Even if you are an individual who lives a minimalist lifestyle, it is not hard for you to venture out and discover a space that is loaded with material possessions. Many times we put a great emphasis on these possessions and cling to them tightly. When one breaks or becomes misplaced, we enter a state of anger, fear, or sadness. In reality, this item likely had nothing to do with our ability to survive. Instead, it was something that we attached happiness to and that we failed to realize the impermanence of. As a result, when it was inevitably removed from our lives, we felt painful emotions.

More than just objects can invoke this feeling within' our lives, though. People, pets and even plants and other living beings all tend to carry profound meanings in our lives. We care deeply for the living beings that we surround ourselves with, and we often forget that they are impermanent as well. Just because someone comes in your life doesn't mean that they will stay. Even if they have been in your life for a lengthy amount of time, it doesn't promise that they will be there forever. Eventually the inevitable will occur and they will be removed from your existence, or you from theirs.

In Western culture, the topic of death is one that is often skirted or avoided altogether. We dislike the idea of impermanence so much that our entire culture avoids it and its meaning. We prefer to ignore the inevitable fate of death. Then, when it inevitably arises, we become profoundly pained, angered and saddened by its occurrence. Due to our fear of impermanence, we suffer even worse when we lose those that we care about. While that is not to suggest that mindfulness will completely change your experience and eliminate the grieving period, it does mean that being mindful will enable you to more thoroughly enjoy your time with said beings and feel deeper gratitude for their company. Then, when the inevitable does happen, you will be able to grieve knowing what you've always known: one way or another, it would end this way. Whether you lost them to death or to a change in life plans and paths, you will grieve, but you will be accepting of this inevitable loss. It will be easier for you to endure than one who never considered it or gave thought to the inevitable experience of loss due to the natural law of impermanence.

"You can't stop the waves, but you can learn to surf."
- Jon Kabat-Zinn

Just as Jon Kabat-Zinn says in the above quote, there truly is no way to stop the inevitable laws of life. Impermanence is one of those laws, and there is nothing that anyone can do to change that or buy extra time. As previously mentioned, we only get so many trips around the sun before our time to move on comes. The best thing you can do is to recognize this and embrace each moment with those people and things that you cherish and love most. This includes yourself, as one day you, too, will pass on. Neither you nor anyone or anything else on this entire planet is permanent. Even the earth itself will one day pass on, making way for new life or existence in the universe.

By learning to ride the waves of life and surf them, you give yourself the best chance to mindfully experience each present moment and gain the most from it that you can. You give yourself the ability to live from a peaceful state of existence and distinguish the possibility for excessive disappointment, grief, anger or sadness that arrives when impermanence proves its truth and takes away what cannot possibly last forever.

Suffering (Dukkha)

The next inevitable mark of existence is suffering and is like impermanence. The word "Dukkha" loosely translates to suffering, but more directly translates to "unsatisfactory" or "imperfect". It is important to realize that suffering exists in everything and everyone. We are all here to experience a degree of suffering on one level or another. Everything that is material and mental with a beginning and an ending and that is composed of the five skandhas (form, sensation, perception, mental formations, and consciousness) and which has not been liberated to Nirvana will be considered Dukkha or suffering. Therefore, even things that are beautiful and elegant and pleasant experiences themselves are dukkha.

Through the Buddha's teachings, we learn that there are three primary states of suffering. The first state of suffering is pain itself, and is translated from dukkhadukkha. This state of suffering encompasses physical, emotional and mental pains. The next type of suffering is suffering relating to impermanence or change. This suffering is translated to "viparinamadukkha". This means that everything that you experience will soon be gone, including happiness. Because of this, you should emphasize your opportunity to enjoy it while it is existing, and prevent yourself from clinging to it so that you don't experience unnecessary pain or when it disappears. The third and final suffering relates to conditioned states. suffering state of This is

translated to " samkharadukkha" and means that we are affected by and dependent on other things. Because of this dependency and these experiences, we are directly affected by them and this causes states of suffering within' us.

Non-Self or Egolessness (Anatta)

The third and final mark of existence is inevitable, as all three marks are. This state is called the non-self or egolessness, and is translated to Anatta, or "anatman" in Sanskrit. This teaching helps you learn that you are not a whole or independent entity. Rather, the ego or the individual self is actually considered to be a byproduct of the five skandhas, which you may remember are form, sensation, perception, mental formations, and consciousness.

The five skandhas give us the illusion that we are a self and that we are individual and separate from all other living beings in this universe. But, just as everything in life, the five skandhas are consistently undergoing change and are also subject to impermanence. The notso-simple truth is that you are not the same for two consecutive moments. Realizing this can be a difficult journey that takes a long time, and in some traditions, it is believed that this is only possible by monks. In life, we naturally cling to who we think we are, and we fail to realize that we are never the same from moment to moment. Just as everything else, we ourselves are impermanent. More so than just the fact that we eventually will die. But also because we change so frequently that we are never the same person for too long in our life.

These three marks of existence are ones that are inevitable in life. There is no possibility for you to eliminate them completely from your life, as they are a fundamental part of life itself. All of the experiences you have in life contribute to one or more of these marks of existence in one way or another. Still, the practice of becoming mindful gives you the opportunity to become deeply aware of these and act with a deeper level of understanding in mind. Instead of living at the mercy of these three marks, you can take them into consideration with your conscious decisions and use them as a guiding factor when you are making decisions in your life. These three marks of existence give you a deeper sense of what your unenlightened experience is, and give you the opportunity to shape your mindset and your life as a result.

Chapter Summary:

• The three marks of existence are present in everyone's life
• The three marks include: Impermanence (Anicca), suffering (dukkha), and not-self or egolessness (Anatta)
• Impermanence teaches that nothing - not even ourselves - are permanent
• Suffering teaches that all life is associated with suffering
• Not-self teaches that we are not whole beings all on our own

Chapter 7: Mindful Self-Transformation

We need to realize that in most of the cases, the cause of the failure is within ourselves. It could be improper planning, it could be lack of proper implementation, or it could even be the complete lack of awareness of what is going on.

Mindfulness not only trains us to be aware of the present experiences but it also helps us identify what went wrong and how. The human nature tends to hold the external factors responsible for the happenings. People often blame the black cat crossing the way, broken mirror, number 13, broken star or even the prophecies from the self-acclaimed fortune tellers.

The problem with the majority of human population is the readiness to accept the influence of something paranormal. The belief that nothing could be done against these factors adds insult to the injury. Wasim Akram, the fast bowler from

Pakistan, was told by a famous Australian palmist that he would die at the age of 36. Wasim, rather than being bothered by the prophecy, continued playing cricket for the next 12 years and even today he is alive and enjoying the life to its full extent. The surprising fact is that Wasim Akram had been the patient of Diabetes since the age of 30 and he never bothered this disease as well. He is fit even today; he never showed any signs of concern, and that is why happiness became his way of life.

The problems with the common people are that when such prophecy denounces, people give it unnecessary importance. The subject becomes the headline of the everyday life of the person as well as of the life of his or her friends and family. So much of mental energy and thought process is consumed for a bluff that people do not find anything else worthy of discussion. We ignore the importance of our lives in such a pathetic manner. We need to change this attitude.

It is vital to realize the responsibility. Check your routine and see what you do and what you should be doing. Do not forget to set the goals and then work hard to meet the ends.

Getting Rid of Bad Habits

You are the supreme creation of God, and you have authority over your decisions and thoughts. You are the guide to your destiny, and this is what mindfulness requires you to accept and realize. Once you realize your own importance, you must figure out what is going on in your life and why certain events are happening.

In this regard, watch your habits which sometimes become close to the instinct because your body and mind become so much associated with some habits. Overcoming a bad habit is one of the most challenging tasks.

A relatively easier way is to replace a bad habit with a good habit. Eradication of a bad habit is almost impossible without engaging the mind in something else. In practical life, if you cannot achieve short-term goals or your performance is not up to the mark, it could be because of your poor time management or laziness. The laziness could be the result of over-sleeping and not doing exercise in the morning. For agility, you need to get up early in the morning, but the problem is that late-rising has become your habit. Think of a solution by introducing something to your mind and body so that the focus shifts from sleeping to early-rising.

You may think of you of your favorite sports and start playing that sports early in the morning. You could think of anything which attracts your mind and body and set the timing of this activity at early morning.

The happening of bad things or the occurrence of bad outcomes is because of your inability to do things in the right way. You need to track the failure first of all and then concentrate on the mistakes. One factor stands out, which is known as inconsistency. For a mindful living, you need to be consistent and focused. It requires a change in your overall attitude. You need to ACT NOW. There is nothing for those who wait. If you are seriously concerned, you have to make a decision and then stand by it come what may.

We need to realize that the bad habits originate from bad choices we make in our lives. If you are a smoker, recall the time when you first smoked. You'll instantly realize that this was the easiest thing to say NO to avoid this habit. A bad choice, probably made instantly, turned into a massive problem for the rest of your life. Think about any bad habit, and you'll find that the role of choice was evident. This is the pattern of our lives. The role of choice is so powerful that we cannot ignore it.

We need to be mindful whenever we come across the situation in which we have to make a choice. When it comes to something like smoking, drinking or anything which our conscience suggests immoral, bad or harmful, be strong to say

NO. This NO should be so firm that nobody should dare offer the choice hence after.

So, the best way to avoid bad habits it to concentrate on the disadvantages right at the time when you are offered with the choice. The lousy fact about our nature is that we assume ourselves to be strong enough to get rid of a habit whenever we want to. This is a fantasy. We make such claims just to trick ourselves. The fact is, when a habit becomes the part of our lives, it becomes increasingly tough to get rid of it.

Mindful Bad-Habit Elimination

•Take a pencil and a diary

•Write down all the bad habits in your personality

•Then check once, whenever you perform that habit (suppose if you smoke a cigarette, check the Smoking Habit once and so on)

•This is the way to track the frequency of the bad habit

- Keep it doing for a week

After one week, check the frequency and count the check marks against each bad habit. This practice will reveal shocking results. The reason is, our instinct tells us to underestimate the frequency of the bad habit. If a person smokes 20 cigarettes a day, he would say he smoked 10 to 12 if he did not keep the record. The record keeping tells you what you are doing and how often. This tracking will trigger a sense of alarm in your mind, and this is the point when you must take action.

For the next week, your brain will automatically try to beat the previous week's tally by reducing the frequency. Automatically, your mind will become aware are more focused. Next week's tally will be low (encouraging) and keep this routine going for as long as you want.

Don't forget to replace the bad habit with a good habit. For instance, for each reduced number of cigarette, you can replace a banana, an apple or any other fruit you love. It is simple, effective and it works!

Changing Relationships

Different stages of life present different relationships. At the time of birth, a kid relates to the mother. Then with the father and siblings. With the passage of time, relatives include in this relationship, and then classmates become friends. In practical life, there is love relationship and colleagues. These relationships require different types of attitude. The challenge is to maintain these relationships in good spirit, and we can only do it if we are mindful.

The problem occurs when another relationship adds. You might have heard the terms Electra complex and Oedipus complex. These terms express the abnormality of the relationships. These occurrences are due to mindless attitude. We need to learn that an individual is born free and has to maintain different relationships with different people, so nobody is bound to stick with only one relationship.

When a relationship is intense, suppose between a mother and the kid, the kid feels jealous of his or her siblings. When we grow old, the jealousy in different relationships becomes evident. A boy in love with a girl does not want the girl to talk to any other male in the world. Things get worse when we keep silent. A mindful person will always talk openly and share the concerns. In this way, there will be a feedback and things can settle as the result of the communication.

In most of the cases, we stay quiet. The other person in the relationship also prefers to stay quiet because of his or her ego. A stage comes that the relationship reduces to "good morning" and "good night"; nothing more than that. This is chaotic, and often people feel that it is too late to negotiate.

We need to accept that this world is full of people and we have to engage with them.

Living in society, interaction is a must. Relationships get hurt because of false assumptions. These days, we see people checking "last seen" and "status" of others, on social media applications. This information doesn't present more than a clue. Our brain comes into play. Here, the thought pattern plays the most important role. People often derive negative conclusions. This practice ruins the whole relationship. People suffer from mental stress, and ultimately it affects their performance in every walk of life.

Life works in its own way, and we cannot bind people according to our wish. Being mindful, we must have a check on our expectations. Just as we cannot do without important relationships, friends, relatives, and colleagues; other also cannot destroy their relationships for good. This simple concept is the key to maintain the relationships in true spirit.

We need to assume the positive aspects and factors. Our positive thinking will help us escape the mental depression and maintain good relationships. On your part, you need to maintain the balance. Sometimes, people like to ignore others over a considerable period just to notice how much they miss them. This technique does not conclude anything because there obviously, every human being doesn't like to be ignored and want a relationship to prosper.

Never forget to watch your words if you want a good relationship. A mindless living is full of foolish talks, aggression, and comments which disgraces the relationship. We often do that without even knowing it. A mindful living must also be focused on our conduct, the way we talk, the words we chose, etc.

Balancing the relationships is important because when you lack this balance, you are actually disturbing a part of your surroundings. Give proper time to your kids and wife. You must visit your parents every weekend. You need to communicate with your parents frequently on the phone because your parents always expect care and you must demonstrate love and care. Your relationship with friends and relatives is also important but keep it to a limit. Do not cut off but do not engage so much that you forget your family and profession. As a professional, your relationship with the colleagues must be formal, clean and ethical. You need to realize the ranks, positions, duties, and rights. But do not become something for granted.

Chapter 8: Active Listening

Listening is another task that we often treat mindlessly. When we talk to other people, we often keep our mind working, trying to create responses to the other person's ideas without truly listening to the entire message of the other person.

As a result, misunderstandings often occur. You also need to be mindful when you are talking to other people. You should observe not only what they are saying but also the little details in their way of communicating.

If you want to achieve mindfulness, you should also train your active listening skills. You should start to do this technique when making unimportant conversations with the people around you. When talking with your coworkers at work for instance, you should employ active listening even when they are just talking about things that are unimportant to you.

Do these steps to achieve mindfulness when listening:

Choose a target that you will listen to. It could be a person or an object with an auditory output.

When that person speaks, you should keep your ears focused on what the person is saying. To support your hearing, you can also keep your eyes on the lips of the other person. The goal is to understand what the other person is saying and to avoid getting distracted by the things around us.

When we are doing small talk, our mind often wanders off because of the distractions around us. Many people have also developed the habit of going through the notifications in our phones when someone is talking. Most of the time, there is nothing important in our phones.

To keep a mindful approach to living, you should practice mindfulness when talking to the people around you. When talking with your kids over breakfast for instance, you should give them your full attention. Instead of reading the paper in silence while you do your breakfast, you should talk to them and listen to them speak. You should ask them questions to encourage them to speak.

You should also be mindful of the body language of the people you are talking to. People often supplement their talk with body language to communicate better. You will understand people better if you also pay attention to the non-verbal cues when they communicate.

If you can do active listening at will, it is a sign that you are in control of your mind. When this skill is developed, you will be able to avoid common distractions that take away your attention from listening.

You should also follow this technique when listening to music. When doing this activity, you should avoid multitasking or entertaining distractions around you. Instead, sit back, relax, and keep your attention focused on the music.

Most people do not do this because they think it is a waste of time. They try to fit as many activities in their schedule as possible. This leads to an extremely stressful lifestyle. By doing this technique, you will be able to block off distractions, decreasing the amount of stress that you experience. In the process, you will also improve your ability to understand the people around you. You will also give them the impression that you are interested in learning more about them.

Chapter 9: Managing Anger With Mindfulness

There are few emotions as disruptive and potentially harmful as anger. Feeling rage or anger not only affects your demeanor, it can cause a great deal of stress. Mindfulness practice can help you manage your feelings of anger in a positive way, enabling you to achieve emotional equilibrium. When you learn how to use mindfulness techniques, you may find you respond to situations optimally, avoiding anger in the first place.

Is anger ever a normal emotion, and when does it become counterproductive?

Anger is an emotion experienced by everyone at some point. It is important to understand the difference between acknowledging a feeling of anger versus responding or acting out of anger. There are many negative effects of anger. Anger is not a constructive part of emotional equilibrium.

Feelings of anger affect not only you those around you, but also your family, friends, and coworkers.Negativity breeds negativity, and feelings of anger increase your risk of stroke, high blood pressure, heart disease and heart attacks. Using equilibrium techniques to successfully handle feelings of anger may be one of the most important things you do for yourself and those you love. Learning to minimize anger and incorporate positivity into your life, achieving emotional equilibrium, has a host of benefits.

How can mindfulness be useful during times of anger?

With practice and training, mindfulness techniques can help you remain aware of your physical responses and your emotional state when you are in a situation in which you react with anger.You are able to be more in tune with your body, and more even in your responses.

It is extremely difficult, and sometimes impossible, to respond to the emotion of anger in the most positive way.It requires deliberate practice to manage powerfully negative emotions like rage and anger.The more adept you are at mindfulness techniques, the easier it will be for you to respond in emotionally positive ways to events and situations, or to handle feelings of anger in the way you feel appropriate to maintain your emotional equilibrium.

Try this mindfulness technique when you find yourself becoming angry!

First, you must be aware that you are feeling anger.It is necessary to focus on the physical sensations you are feeling.Anger invokes such a strong response that often your mind is not aware of your body as a coping mechanism.Acknowledge the physical symptoms including your heartbeat, your face, tension in your muscles, how your stomach feels, even how you are breathing.

Now you need to turn your focus to your breathing.Concentrate on breathing in, and sending that breath to one of the areas you are experiencing a physical reaction to your anger.Close your eyes and cleanse that part of your body with the breath.Count each of your breaths up to ten.Each time you release your breath, visualize yourself releasing anger from your body.

Be aware of the way you feel as you take each breath, as well as how you feel from each physical manifestation of your anger. Focus on these sensations as they become more or less intense, and acknowledge and accept them.

Now you are ready to be more introspective, turning from your physical state and concentrating instead on your thoughts.You are not judging your thoughts.You are noticing them, accepting them, and allowing them to flow through your mind.Do not focus on the thoughts themselves.You are only acknowledging them.

Using this anger management mindfulness technique will release most of your anger.As your anger diminishes, you will be able to more clearly evaluate your situation, and what, if any, action you should take.It is important to acknowledge your anger when you feel it, and to manage it in a positive way using the techniques you are practicing.

How consistent do I need to be to achieve results?

Although you don't have to practice every mindfulness technique on a daily basis, it is useful to practice mindfulness technique to achieve emotional equilibrium daily.It takes practice to master, like any skill, and the more confident and knowledgeable you are about utilizing this technique, the better you will be able to control, prevent, or handle anger when you feel it.

It is better to practice mindfulness techniques for resolving anger before you are in a situation where you are angry.The better prepared you are, the easier it will be to acknowledge and release feelings of anger.It also becomes easier to understand and analyze the situation which caused you to become angry to start with.Consistent practice, and the use of the mindfulness technique whenever you feel angry, will enable you to maintain your emotional equilibrium.

Chapter 10: Rain – A Four-Step Process For Using Mindfulness In Difficult Situations.

Ait has been tested and applied by many people, and is really a awesome step to begin with.

Here are the four steps:

1:**R** –**R**ecognize what it happening.

2:**A** –**A**llow life to be just as it is.

3:**I** – **I**nvestigate the inner experience.

4:**N** –**N**on-identification.

Explaining RAIN:

R – Recognizing and litreally stopping at the moment, taking a deep breath and seeing the emotion arising, from what it is arising and from where it is arising, and just being there to observe it, and name it.

'OK, I am feeling a little heavy.' It all happens in the **present** moment. Take a deep breath, come into the moment and see for yourself – what are you feeling? A sense of being relaxed? When a second ago you felt a little heavy? It may even have started working already.

A – Allow. Allowing means to accept the present like it is. When we accept the present moment as it is, we give an opportunity to form a second opinion, a second chance, for seeing how we can get out of a situation. Be detached and take it on with a new level of enthusiasm and with greater understanding. When that breakthrough happens, you will see that you **grow**. And one of the greatest things our spirit, our soul, our energy – whatever you want to call it, whatever it is that allows us to transcend – has is a sense of **growing**.. This is what it means to 'Allow' – give it a try yourself, right now. Just stop, and allow yourself to accept the current moment as it is, and you will see how easily it sinks in, and how it is happening right now. And you will see, and I beg you to see, that the very basic part of life is this concept. Once you start to become mindful, you begin to grow, and stop wandering off to useless things. Take full charge of the inner you, your inner child, and you can follow it wherever it takes you. For only you are your own master.

The third step is the most interesting and should be used with responsibility – the

I, Investigation. Now you should understand that the first two processes of Recognition and Allowing serve to make the problem and the emotion subside. But trust me, we are living in a world where there are only two things: to live peacefully, and to solve problems so that we can live peacefully. Sometimes simply allowing things, the simple acceptance of the thing, makes it subside and makes us relaxed. Like in a relationship, for example, if a boyfriend and girlfriend have an argument, and the boy really loves the girl, he has accepted, 'ok, we are in a fight.' He has accepted it, and is now relaxed, but the question now is that he has another problem in front of him to be with her or not? Now we have to detach ourselves from the problem by asking this question:

"It is not my problem – so what is the permanent solution?"

In other words, you need to get the simple understanding that the problem is not yours. Straight away, ask this simple question: What's the permanent solution? And after this, let the mind effortlessly go wherever it wants to go, and it will give you signals –ok, I have to do this, I have to watch this video, I have to go learn this, I have to go and buy flowers – the only thing that happens between that and this is the actions. You need to take action on those, and believe me, if you have no ego, and understand that there is one single mindfulness on this Earth, and you take that action – you will have an amazing life. Not only in relationships, every aspect of life..

And the last point,

N – Non-identification. I can't emphasize non-identification enough – I have suffered a lot! Your relationships suffer, your work suffers – everything suffers simply because of identifying yourself with problems, or with somebody else's problems. Try to get this into your gut: You are not your thoughts, you are just your emotions. I'll give you an example – I just had to do this work of mine, and I wasn't ever able to do it because I had the thought in my mind that I had never done it, so I never could do it. And if I could have seen that I am not my thoughts, which is the only truth – the present is the truth – if I had done that? I would have understood my emotions – it is not the present that is creating the emotions, it is just the thoughts of the past that are creating the emotions – and I would have let go with the help of love inside me, and I would simply have come out of it. You will know if you have learnt to swim – many people are petrified to even touch the water. Does that mean they can't learn to swim?

It is a stupid misunderstanding that anything in the past has to be connected with the present and the future. It's simple – you can conquer anything on this Earth. And if you don't believe me, there are people on this Earth who have been in far worse situations than you have ever been in –trust me on that. If you search on Google, you can see plenty of people in far worse shit than you, so don't tell me that you are in the most difficult situation. It is simple. You will find an answer. Do this in difficult times and you will come out of it – come what may.

Chapter 11: Body Scan Technique

The method of the body scan mindfulness exercise is just to notice your body. It's not really about relaxing the body; however, this is often a side effect of the practice. It's just about being aware of the body and the present moment. Usually, the response to bodily pain and discomfort is to distract yourself or try to numb the pain. In this exercise, you'll accept and notice that pain with curiosity.

1.Lie down or sit in a comfortable position and make sure that you don't have any constrictions. Loosen any tight clothing like jeans, blouses, or just wear a pair of sweat pants and a loose t-shirt during this exercise.

2.Start with the feet and pay attention to the physical feelings in them, such as discomfort, pain, coolness, tension, warmth, tightness, or anything else that might be happening. Just pay attention to the physical sensations and feelings. Don't judge them as being negative or positive, or try to change them. Just be aware of them.

3.Now let your awareness drift up from the feet to your shins and calves, again just paying attention to the physical sensations in those areas of your body, including pain, discomfort, or tightness. Then allow your awareness to drift up the body, doing the same with a gentle noticing for all the different parts of the body, such as thighs, hips, behind, genital region, abdomen, chest, lower back, upper back, hands, fingers, lower arms, upper arms, neck, shoulders, head, temples, forehead, face, cheeks, eyes, nose, jawline, and mouth.

4.Then allow that awareness to drift slowly and gently back down the body, observing any other places where there's tension, pain, or discomfort. Go all the way back down to the feet.

5.Keep doing this exercise for around five minutes. It can be done while you're sitting in a chair or lying down somewhere comfortably. Over time, you shouldn't worry about how long it takes. Just let yourself pay attention to your body's feelings. If thoughts intrude as you're doing this exercise, that's alright. Just notice them and allow them to drift away. Bring your awareness back to your body.

One of the variations of this exercise is to do this in front of a mirror and focus on the parts of the body that you're not comfortable with. Do this and notice your thoughts and emotions as you look at every part of your body.

Chapter 12: Relieve Stress, Self – Improvement And Self-Control With Meditation

The craft of Meditation has been around for more than 5,000 years. Figuring out how to ponder legitimately takes sooner or later; in any case, anybody can get a handle on the essential ideas in only a brief while compass. You would start with the essential frame and figure out how to unwind; wipe everything insane and turning your consideration regarding one and only single thought. The word Meditation is an intends to allude to numerous otherworldly practices.

Reflection gives a man a superior concentrate on mindfulness, a higher condition of awareness, and the capacity to accomplish a more inventive perspective. It has been polished by a wide range of religions and societies from each nation on the planet, including the western world.

It has experienced much feedback numerous specialists, on the grounds that there was no evidence that it lived up to expectations. On the other hand, there have numerous studies done on Meditation and the discoveries were incredible. Specialists and individuals all over the place observed that it does help a man assuage stretch and agony and in addition it helps the individual to have a vastly improved life.

Numerous individuals experience the ill effects of anxiety from their employments, anxiety of a circumstance they may be in, or from a sickness. Contemplation aides diminish this anxiety, and torment from some type of disease by centering your considerations far from your inconveniences. Healing centers and facilities have utilized this method all the more as a part of the western world since the 1960's, and it has turn out to be popular to the point that it is being offered by numerous organizations, as an out-of-office class. A large portion of the members are taught to sit with folded legs, be that as it may, not a wide range of Meditation are taught this; a wide range of conventions may have different approaches to Meditate. Some may need you to sit on a stool. Some essential ideas in every one of the conventions incline toward that you hold your back absolutely straight, and utilize an ommmm sound core interest.

One approach to practice a type of Meditation is to rests and clear your psyche by envisioning a gleaming shining cloud out in space voyaging towards earth. As it achieves earth, it stops and the sparkling shines frame a light emission directly over your nation, then the light emission moves descending toward your city to you and as it gets to you, it starts to enter the highest point of your head. All of a sudden, you can feel a shivering feeling going down your body from your head. As this shivering feeling moves down, you will start to feel a warm feeling where the light emission is going through your body. You will feel the shivering go on down warming your body in every part until it guides itself out through your toes. Your body will feel just as it is as yet beating a surge of molecule light, and you will feel casual and brimming with vitality.

This strategy is one that I have actually utilized for a long time. It has improved my life. I figured out how to reject the resentment that I had such a large amount of, and it taught me a lot more.

Chapter 13: Tips For Practicing The Meditation

A couple of years back, for the most part of my life, I was going through very hard & sad times. I was utilizing an ample amount of time inside my own head. I was not in control of my mind. I was just not able to switch it off, when I really wanted it to be off.

My mind kept droning and my body was completely exhausted. I was surrounded by the feelings like I was going to be crazy. I started reading plenty of things about meditation as I was so desperate to search a way out. I wanted to take the control back in my life. Even after taking a few meditation sessions, I was not able to make it work for me. It took a lot of time and was very hard. So finally, I decided to give up.

Then somewhere back in 2015, as a part of my psychotherapy training, I attended a course related to "Mindfulness" that introduced me to a fresh approach of living mindfully— a much easier way that actually was working for me. It would surely would work for you, as well. We just have to know the exact meaning of mindfulness.

Jon Kabt-Zinn, the professional, reminds us that there is no perfect way to practice mindfulness, there is alsono "standard" way to judge yourself. So, when your mind strolls, don't get disappointed or upset. You just need to bring your mind back frequently and gently. In old-style mindfulness, while sitting with closed eyes and observing the breath, we were trained to perform all this. Especially for beginners, this is really very hard to perform, as they sit observing their breath, their thoughts level repeatedly seem to get bigger. In addition to that, once it's completed, you still have to return to the life that you often find obstacles in.

For most of us, the definition of relaxation is to sit in front of the television towards the end of day full of stress. However, stress is to damaging to simply minimize as best as you can. Rather, you must learn how to counter stress, and learn to heal your body and mind. To effectively counter stress, we are supposed to trigger the natural relaxation response of the body. We can perform this by putting into practice techniques that helps us relax such as meditation, deep breathing, yoga and rhythmic exercise. We can reduce everyday stress by fitting such activities in your life in order to improve on mood and energy.

Meditation that leads to mindfulness has been recommended by many experts to minimize stress.

It doesn't matter if your nearby environment is busy, loud or you are at work. You can still perform mindfulness meditation. You may change your consciousness for any crucial interruptions, and come back to mindfulness type easily. You may begin with small 3 to 5 minute activities, just like when you brush your teeth.

You will likely see your anxiety reducing immediately, so you may use this technique as a fast stress management plan, and obviously for long term development. For practicing mindfulness, you can practice at all times in the day, whether you are busy or not. You do not need to find long periods of time in your day to practice this technique.

Past this point are the techniques through which you would be able to practice the meditation to Eliminate Fear, Stress and Anxiety within 30 Minutes:

Choosing a best place for you to meditate:

You need to choose the best place for yourself, where you can meditate comfortably. Perfect characteristics of a good meditation place consist of someplace neither too light nor too dark, and neither too cold nor too hot. You also should avoid any place which is likely to have distractions or disturbances. You do not have to perform this at home, if you feel another place is more suitable to your liking.

A quiet place at your home is a great way to start with however; going to a meditation centre close by your home is great as well.

If you are not able to meditate or don't feel safe in the place you are in, change locations.

Deciding an appropriate posture:

Believe me it's not that difficult.You can easily decide a suitable posture.Every posture has its own advantages & disadvantages, so until you are more aware &practiced at examining what's going on, it is always suggested to study one posture at a time. Decide and check the type of posture that suits you - it could be anything like sitting, standing, lying down, or even walking. As a beginner, it's good to stick to one posture because it will help you stick to a regimen. Make sure you pick a position that is comfortable for you!

Reclining posture: This posture is also known as the lion posture over and over again. In this posture, the left hand rests on top of your body (left side) and you need to lie down on your right hand side with your head resting on a small pillow, or your right hand.

It is suggested to try another style, if this position causes your body's circulation to become worse. For beginners, lying on your back is a common method, but it may frequently encourage drowsiness.

Standing posture:since it's an upright posture, you may raise your hands with palms facing you at a comfortable angle and height (to find a comfortable pose where you can hang your hands with minimal tension and effort, you may have to adjust your arms), or down by your side.

You should never lock your knees and your feet should be your shoulder width apart with equally dispersed weight.

Relax your lower back and stomach.

Walking posture: Though it has a few disadvantages, it is likely the best posture for implementing mindfulness meditation into your busy life. It's a type of posture that makes mindfulness the easiest to fit in your everyday experiences. Walking is normally done over a small distance at a slow gentle pace. It is best performed in a non-distracting and secluded area.

You can focus on the intention to move as well as various parts of your body like the chest, the hips, the feet and the legs.

You can clasp your hands gently or by your side.

Seated posture: In this posture you can choose whatever makes you feel most comfortable. A few variations have the legs folded with one leg on the other also called"half lotus", some have them crossed, or some of the variations have both the legs folded with the feet facing up, also called as"complete lotus". Typically, lotus postures are only for the most advanced practitioners, as the average person is not quite flexible enough to sit in that posture.

The palms may be facing up with the fingers either gently touching the thumb relaxed, or the palms can be facing downwards and resting on your legs.

The stomach and lower back should be relaxed and the chest should be open and upright.

Your hands may be resting on your knees or thighs, or folded on your lap gently.

To open the airways, the head should be gently tilted upward and the neck should be balanced.

Visualization Meditation

Guided imagery also known as visualization meditation is an adaption on customary meditation which needs individuals to effectively use not only the visual sense, however also the senses of sound, smell, touch and taste. When visualization is utilized as a technique for relaxation, it includes imagining scenery where you sense solitude and peace, ready to get rid of all anxiety fear and tensions.

Whatever setting happens to be calming and peaceful to you is to be chosen, whether bedroom, garden beach or worship place. Visualization exercise has to be practiced alone and away from distractions, however you may listen to soothing music or listen to a guided visual meditation audio (which you can find on YouTube). Guided meditation audio's are excellent for beginners, however you do not want to rely on them for long periods of time, as you will not have these recordings everywhere you go.

In order to practice visualization, we need to select a secluded and quite setting. During the visualization meditation few of the beginners fall asleep hence it is advised to sit or stand to avoid the same.

Let your tensions and worries leave you by closing your eyes. Visualize a quiet and restful setting. Imagine the place as graphically and realistically as you may can everything that can be seen, heard, smelt or felt. When you put to practice as many physical details as you can, visualization technique works the best, by using a minimum of three of the senses. When doing so, select an imagery which attracts or appeals to yourself; avoid selecting settings or images because somebody has recommended them. Allow your own setting and images to grow and work.

As you have a habit to explore the peaceful imaginary setting, let it engulf you slowly and enjoy the deep relaxation feeling.

After you feel your meditation has come to an end, either because the timer you set has ended or because you can just **feel** that it's over, gently and slowly open your eyes and wake up, doing your best to remain present. Do not try so hard to remain present that you feel it is straining you, or you feel like you are forcing it and getting agitated. Simply do your best and understand that you will drift in and out of the present moment, especially if you're a beginner.

You may forget where you are while deep in this meditation practice. In this case, do not worry, and simply trust that you decided to engage in this technique in a place where you feel very comfortable.

It is quite normal. You may feel strange feelings that you have never felt before during this meditation experience. Understand that they are all beneficial experiences, and are a sign that your meditation experience is advancing.

Chapter 14: Mindful Meditation

This is a very valuable lesson to learn and something that you need to make room for every day of your life. Thus, don't expect to give an hour to it because you may not have the time every day. Repetition is very important because when you engage in something every day on a regular basis, it becomes a habit and there is no healthier habit than meditation. Put aside about ten minutes a day at the beginning and remember that you can use meditation during the course of your day as well if you need to, to help to make things clearer. Here are the benefits of meditation:

- Your blood pressure is lowered

- Your heart beat is slower

- You are more prone to relax than to stress

- You are tapping into your natural energy

- It clears your mind

- It opens up awareness

People who meditate on a regular basis find that their lives are more fulfilled. They are happier people and can use all of the extra mental energy that they derive from meditation to help make their lives more fulfilling. Say, for example, you have a meeting today with people you want to impress. If you worry about this meeting, you arrive with that hesitance that is natural when trying to impress someone. However, if you meditate before the meeting instead of worrying, you arrive self-assured and have clear ideas about how to present whatever it is that you need to present. Meditation is clarity and believe me, it will change the way that you look at your life.

You will need to allot a certain space in your home for meditation. This helps you to take the activity more seriously and to devote ten minutes daily to the activity. There is a system called habit stacking.

This is where you tag a new habit to an old one and make sure that you perform that new habit every day. At first, it will be intentional and you will have to make the effort to let the new habit in. However, after you have done this for a period of between 31 days and a month and a half, the habit is so engrained that you do it without any mental effort whatsoever. This habit stacking is a wonderful way to introduce meditation into your daily life.

The best time of day to meditate will either be first thing in the morning before you go to work and before the mind is confused by the hustle bustle of life or in the evening before the evening meal. You can choose to have both of these times devoted to meditation if you think that this will be helpful to you. So, look at a habit you have in the morning and tag the new meditation habit to it as shown below:

- Get out of bed
- Go to the bathroom

- Meditate
- Have breakfast

You need to make a definite slot for this new activity and the reason that people meditate each day is that they get better at it as time passes and thus it becomes more effective. You don't need any special gear to meditate, but if you are fit and healthy, it may be an idea to have a firm cushion to sit on to support your body, if you choose to sit on a cushion on the floor. In this position, you must keep your back straight, bend your knees and cross your ankles. If you can't get down onto the floor, then use a hard chair and sit up straight with your feet planted flat on the floor.

Grounding

Basically this means making yourself comfortable and finding the position that you can stay in and feel comfortable in during the course of your meditation. Ten minutes may not sound like a long time, but believe me, if you have not grounded yourself into a comfortable position, it can seem like a lot longer as you fight with cramp or pain in your back. Thus, when you are sitting on the cushion, sway to the left and right until you feel that your body is perfectly comfortable. The grounding when you are on a chair is having your feet flat on the floor. This gives you the stability that you need.

Timing

You should never meditate with a full stomach because the digestive processes will interrupt your comfort and get in the way of your meditation practice. Early morning before breakfast is perfect as is early evening before the evening meal.

Breathing

I have spoken briefly about breathing, but as you close your eyes, you need to get the rhythm of your breathing regular. Thus follow the pattern shown below:

Breathe in to the count of eight

Breathe out to the count of ten

Carry on breathing in this way until you feel the rhythm is solid and you are breathing in a regular manner and are able to keep to that rhythm. This deep breathing has been explained and it is beneficial when you are meditating. The Buddhist monks do this but they may not need the counting because they are so accustomed to breathing in this manner that they know instinctively the length of each breath. At this stage, you are just beginning, so will not be so familiar with the breathing routine. Thus, keep breathing until you feel that you are doing this automatically almost without even thinking of the counting.

Meditating

Often people ask me what meditation is and it's quite easy to explain. It is separating your mind and your thoughts from the regular world that you live in and simply concentrating on the breathing. Thus, you need a calm place to do this, where the mind will not be distracted at all. When you are more experienced you will be able to do this regardless of your surroundings, but for the time being, you need that peace and quiet to concentrate. While you are breathing, think only of the breath. Feel the breath coming into your body from the nostrils and you can even imagine it as a huge flame of life that is going deep inside you. Then, when you breathe out, make it purposeful and follow the breath as it leaves your body. Think of nothing else at all.

There may be times when you find that there is outside influence. For example, a ray of sunshine may just grab your attention as it pours in through the window. You may hear traffic outside and find that your attention is drawn toward it. Don't worry too much about this happening. You do need to be in a quiet place when you are first learning, but it's not at all unusual to hear or see things that distract you. What you do need to learn is to simply go back to the moment and back to your concentration on being in that moment with your breath.

The mistake that a lot of people make is that they beat themselves up for having too many thoughts while they are trying to concentrate on meditation. Meditation isn't like trying to stand on your head. The effort should be minimal. The reason it seems so hard at the moment is that you are accustomed to thinking all of the time. What you are doing when you meditate is simply transferring your thoughts so that they are concentrated upon your breath. If thoughts creep in, don't get upset about it. Simply dismiss the thoughts and go back to doing what it is you were doing.

When you are training the mind to be quiet, it's not natural and of course it will give you difficulty at first because you are accustomed to having a mind filled with thoughts. You are in effect closing the boxes that hold all those thoughts and rising above them so that you can gain some spiritual awareness that you usually cannot see because your head is too filled to brimming with worries and stresses. You don't even have to program your meditation to sort out particular problems. The fact that you are letting go of worldly thought means that your subconscious can go to work on real problems without you being conscious of it and the clarity that you get from meditation is wonderful. You may not feel it straight away, but when you have been practicing it for a while, you will really notice that you are calmer and that your approach to problems in life is less strained.

Breathe in to the count of eight

Breathe out to the count of ten

Little by little you get so involved in the breathing process that you are able to drop all of your worldly worries and simply allow your mental energy to be used on concentrating on the breath. Don't expect it to come easily because it's a little like training your mind to close down and relax. Just as it was difficult for you to relax before the relaxation exercise, so you will find that your mind isn't quite ready for this jump from conscious thinking to conscious rest. It takes time but it does happen and each session that you have improves your ability to let go of all things worldly and simply allow the mind to avoid that overload of information that everyone experiences in their everyday life.

Concentrated Meditation

When you are able to meditate with your eyes closed, you can open your eyes but for this exercise, it pays to have something inspirational to concentrate on while you are meditating. If you have ever been to a Buddhist temple, you will find that altars are beautifully illustrated with soft colors and statues. The Buddhists are not worshipping idols. The altars are simply used to inspire the Buddhists to be able to meditate. Thus, if you can create your own little inspirational area, you will be able to use this for concentrated meditation. This is a type of meditation that allows you to use your senses. Therefore having a scented candle will awaken your sense of smell and sight. Having a picture that warms your heart will help you to sense an atmosphere of wellbeing. It's all about your feelings rather than your thoughts.

Start to breathe in the same way as you did in the last meditation exercise. The counting method is something that helps you to get the breaths regular and gives you something to concentrate on, although in this case, you can use your eyes, your nose and your sense of wellbeing to embrace the atmosphere that you have created. There is nothing quite as wonderful as doing this kind of meditation on an empty beach and feeling the atmosphere of the seaside as well as seeing the wonders of nature in front of you. It takes your mind to another plane, where you stop thinking about the stresses of life and simply think of the breath, the aroma, the sight, the sounds and anything that touches your senses, including taste. Different atmospheres taste differently. You may not be aware of it in your day to day life, but all of your senses are there to help you to grasp the world around you and if you choose this form of meditation, the concentration is on the breath and the awareness of your senses.

Why it's called concentrated meditation or guided meditation is because you don't move your head around to look at what's all around you. Instead, you are guided toward whatever it is that you have decided to concentrate on – whether that's a flame of a candle or a blossom freshly picked from the garden. You are switching off from the world for these moments devoted to meditation and that object that you are observing is simply an extension of that. Thus try to choose something still, so that your concentration is not impaired by interruptions or movements.

After Meditation

This is a time when your heart beat will be slower and your blood pressure will certainly have gone down. Thus, never rise quickly after meditation to go back into your hectic world. Come around slowly and use this period of time to make notes in a journal. This helps you to be more aware and you can write into the journal the things that you believe you can do next time you meditate to help you to improve the meditation process. You could also use the journal simply to record your thoughts in this moment following meditation.

Chapter 15: The Heart Of The Rose Meditation Technique

This is one of the most popular mindfulness meditation techniques in the west. Buddhist monks have been practicing this technique for centuries, but Robin Sharma introduced this to the west through his book, "The Monk Who Sold His Ferrari". This technique is a form of mindful awareness. It helps you pay attention to details. This technique also helps you live in the present moment.

For this exercise, you'll need a rose or any type of flower.

Sit in a comfortable position and how the flower. Then take deep breaths. Inhale through your nose and exhale through your mouth. As you inhale and exhale, notice how your chest goes up and down with every breath.

After ten breaths, shift your attention to the rose. What's the color of the rose? Is it red, white, or yellow? Is it fresh or is it wilting? Is it small or is it large? Take time to notice all the petals. Do you see lines on the petals? Take time to appreciate each curve and each petal.

Then, shift your attention to the center of the rose. What can you see? Pay attention to each curve. Notice each petal curled up to the center of the flower. Just stare at the center of the rose for three to five minutes. If a distracting thought enters your mind, acknowledge that thought and gently release it without judgment.

Then, after your meditation time, say a silent prayer of gratitude and then go about your day.

This technique is difficult, especially if you have an untrained or a restless mind. This will take you a couple of weeks to master so you have to be patient with yourself. You can also set an alarm so that you don't have to look at the clock while you are doing the practice. You can do this for two to three minutes for the first few minutes and then you can increase your meditation time as you progress.

The Heart of the Rose meditation technique is challenging, but it is very beneficial. It helps reduce stress and tension in your body. This technique also sharpens your mind and improves your critical thinking and decision-making skills. This mindfulness practice also helps increase emotional intelligence and it is an effective way to alleviate the symptoms of anxiety.

Chapter 16: Neural Pathways

You need to do this at the level of sensation because the thoughts kick in so fast, they just take over. This is very hard to do, to keep it in the sensation rather than thinking about the sensations. This is very difficult. So you can try this out in small things in your meditations. If you get bored, the difficulty is boredom. If you get restless, the difficulty is restlessness. If you have a headache, that's the difficulty.

You must realize what the first arrow is and, instead of firing a second arrow, instead of thinking about it or even running away from it, you can try to approach it with a kind and friendly curiosity. You can try to go towards the pain. Realize where it comes from. Where it starts in your body, where it spreads to. Remember, pay attention, on purpose, in the present moment, without judgement. Don't choose the big things, choose the very small things.Each time your brain does that it learns a new skill. The neural pathway in the brain becomes more established.

Your brain changes each time you approach something difficult. That mechanism in the brain, that neural pathway becomes more usable. Is like clearing a path in the forest. If you keep walking down it, it stays open. If no one walks that path, it becomes overgrown in a short time. So the more you walk down that path in the brain, the easier it becomes, and when you need it, it's there. Remember that commitment to the practice is the key.

When you meditate, if you take your awareness or attention to the physical sensations of sadness, anger, frustration, boredom, or restlessness, if you take your attention to where you feel those echoes or those emotions in your body, you don't fire the second arrow. You keep it where it is.

If you keep the attention on the sensations associated with the emotion you don't add any more fuel to the fire, you don't add any more arrows. So, patiently, with kindness, observe your sensations using your breath as a guide.

It all only makes sense when you actually experience it. For this reason, you are going to do another exercise which is a short meditation practice. For this practice you should chose a time of the day when you know you will be receptive to calming and stillness.

We all run through the day doing lots of things and don't give ourselves much time to really feel, but for this meditation you must find time to dedicate to listen to what your mind and body are telling you.

Exercise – Mindfulness Meditation

Guidance for Posture and Comfort

To start your meditation, you must be aware of your posture. Bring yourself into a sitting posture that feels awake and dignified.

The spine must be long and tall and the head must be balanced on top of the spine. Roll the shoulders up and back. Place your hands on the knees or thighs. You should be in a wakeful, alive, and comfortable position.

Changing the posture signals a new intention. It's a signal to yourself that you're going to do something to try to work with the stress, to try to respond to stress.

Practice while you read. After you read and learn this meditation, start practicing with your eyes closed.

Time to "BE"

Begin to settle, giving yourself a bit of quality time to just "BE", and as far as possible letting go of whatever has come before or whatever is coming after this moment.

Give yourself this time to simply be there, with an intention to use the breath movements in your body to help you stay present and open to your experience moment by moment.

Bring your attention to the breath

Gently bring your awareness to your breath. Pull all of your focus inwards, into the center of your own being. Inhale fully feeling the lungs. Exhale much more slowly. You are working not to watch the breath but to really feel the breath. Your breath is always with you, so you can use it as an anchor to the present moment at any time. Breathe in deeply through the nose. Soft and long exhale.

Whenever you notice that the mind has been wandering, you may gently comeback to your breath, without judgement. Thoughts come and go. You can let them be and let them go. Do not identify yourself with them. Just let them pass like clouds in the sky and go back to your breath.

Bring your attention to the mind

Bring your attention to your mind. What is happening in your mind right now? There is no need to focus on meditation. What you're trying to do is to notice whatever is there. You gradually create a little bit more stability in the mind, but there is no need to try too hard to focus. The mind will come and go and that's okay. Mindfulness just needs a little bit of steadiness in order to see what's going on in your mind.

Bring your attention to the feelings

Bring your attention to the sensations and feelings in your body. What feelings do you have? Do you feel any pain or tightness? Cold or heat? Lightness or heaviness? Or do you just feel peaceful and pretty quiet? Whatever it is that you might be feeling, where does it feel in the body? Which parts of the body reflect your feelings right now? Where do these feelings start? Maybe in the head? In the chest? And where in the body do they spread to? Try to approach these feelings. Don't run away from them. Don't ignore them. Don't resist them. Don't try to change anything. Just acknowledge whatever is there.

Work with feelings

Explore what happens during this process. How do your thoughts and feelings affect your physical body? Really, be with yourself. Go towards your feelings with friendly curiosity. See if you can be with them rather than denying them. See if you can bring your breath to that place where you feel unease. Imagine the breath can go around those places. Don't try to change anything. Don't try to get rid of it for the moment, just hold it in your awareness. All you are doing is letting the breath meet the difficulty. Gently meeting it as it is. So in a sense, accepting it's there with the in-breath and the out-breath, and not expecting it to change at all. In a sense, what you are learning to do is to be with something difficult. Learning a different strategy to work with stress. A strategy that's a little bit more kind towards the difficult thing.

In the meditation practice, you cultivate acceptance by taking each moment as it comes and being with it fully, as it is. You try not to impose your ideas about what you should be feeling, or thinking, or seeing in your experience. If you keep your attention focused on the present, you can be sure that whatever you are attending to in this moment will change, giving you the opportunity to practice accepting whatever it is that will emerge in the next moment. This meditation is about learning to ask questions and learning to answer them for yourself.

If you have already learned how to do this meditation and have started to practice it with your eyes closed, when you finish it, gently prepare yourself to come back to your awareness, by smoothly opening your eyes, looking to the ground, and then looking in front.

 Self-Reflection

How was this meditation practice for you?

What did you notice for yourself?

Did you have many thoughts?

Did you have mostly nice thoughts or difficult thoughts?

When thoughts came into your mind, how did that affect the feeling of relaxation?

What happened when you woke up to having thoughts?

Was this practice easy or hard?

The purpose of this meditation is not to indulge difficulty, but to learn how to meet difficulties. If you can offer difficult feelings your direct attention in the body, rather than your thoughts about them, that can often be very helpful. So if you feel unease in your chest, if you bring your breath to that place, it could be helpful.

You are just beginning to learn this new skill. It's a difficult one. I encourage you to take it easy and just do a little bit at a time. Allowing difficult things to be in your awareness and using your breath to carry a sense of love and care to those places. Clearly there is wisdom in cultivating acceptance.

Mindfulness Meditation Exercise Summary

Mind the posture

Time to "BE" – Let go of thoughts.

Bring your attention to the breath – Your breath is the anchor to keep you grounded.

Bring your attention to the mind – See what is happening in your mind.

Bring your attention to the feelings – See what you feel. Where the feeling starts and where they spread to in your body.

Work with feelings – How do the feelings affect your body? Go towards the feelings without trying to change anything. Accept your experience just as it is.

Tips to Remember!

- Choose a time and place where you will not be disturbed. Have a date with yourself!

- Don't judge what you are doing and how you are feeling. Just take the experience as it is.

- Acknowledge when you become distracted by the thoughts and come back to the senses.

Chapter 17: Mindful Observation

Life today is fast-paced and full of stress-inducing activities such as working, dealing with other human beings, traffic, bills, money and an unending list of things we deal with during our every moment. When one becomes aware, moment by moment, of one's surroundings it helps to enable coping skills with the difficult thoughts and feelings that may cause stress and anxiety every day of one's life.

When we practice these mindful exercises on a regular basis, we are taken off of auto-pilot where we just react to things that happen and harness the ability to adapt and deal with the challenges we face in a clear-minded, assertive and calm manner.

Stress has a way of making us doubt our own abilities. Anxiety holds us captive and we fall into the pattern of negative thinking. In turn, we set self-limits and question the decisions and actions we take. Mindfulness will help us all be more fully in the moment, and free us to be positive, compassionate, and understanding individuals, not only to ourselves but to others as well.

The next technique we are going to examine, and practice is called mindful observation. This is an open eye where you look intently on any object without moving your eyes. It is a practice in both being still and seeing things like you are looking at them for the first time.

The ancient cultures call it Trataka and believe that your gaze on the object should be direct and intentional, but not strained or forced. It may sound odd, but you shouldn't be concentrating or doing anything that requires effort on your part. You're just gently resting your attention and awareness on an object that you've chosen to observe.

The object of this exercise is to become more aware of the object you are looking at and, in addition, it's exercising your brain and its ability to take in the context, if you will, of what you are looking at with a relaxed approach. It is believed that this type of meditation helps to develop the curious and inquisitive part of your brain.

For this exercise, you will sit on the floor or chair in a comfortable position after choosing an object to observe. You won't be handling the object in any way. You will simply be looking at it.

This meditation has the same mindful awareness we discussed previously, but the eyes will be open. Some practitioners use a candle, others use artwork, mystical words, and letters, or soul gazing. Soul gazing is when one person stares into the eyes of another person in an intimate way.

The benefits of these practices include self-awareness, decreased stress, reduced anxiety and depression as well as increased creativity, confidence and patience.

Benefits

- Willpower: It does take some effort to keep your eyes focus on a single object for some time. Our eyes naturally want to wander and by not allowing them to do so by gently nudging them back to the object, the mental fortitude and willpower will naturally increase.

- Stress Reduction: If you focus your attention on a specific task, your conscious mind tends to disengage from other thoughts such as worry and concerns. This is like your mind and body are taking a well-deserved vacation from stressors and will help to decrease the signs and symptoms of overload, such as lower blood pressure and increase in quality of sleep.

- Thought Awareness: As you stare at the meditation object, your thoughts will continue to move in their normal ebb and flow. This is a great opportunity to focus on the thoughts and emotions going through your mind. One thing to point out is that when the eyes start to stray from the object, so do the thoughts.

☐Gratitude: You will be able to see and be more aware of the virtues and qualities of what you have chosen. Whether a candle's flame, a flower, or a spot on the wall, you will find yourself being more grateful for what you have. Gratitude is an awesome emotion and has been proven to change lives and have numerous health benefits.

Gratitude is simple but is often overlooked as an emotion. But increased gratitude will also increase your mental strength, self-esteem, better mental health, less depression, and anxiety, and even sleep better at night.

Equipment Checklist:

☐ Comfortable chair or cushion where sitting with spine erect is possible

☐A quiet and private place where you will not be disturbed

☐Timer. (again, if you decide to use your phone make sure that notifications are off and set to vibrate if you find you cannot turn it off)

☐ Meditation notebook, pen and/or pencil

☐ A meditation object, such as a burning candle or other objects to use as a focal point

Procedure:

Choosing your meditation object is important. It can be something of importance to you if you wish, an everyday object, a candle, a flower. Informal meditation, there is usually candle with a holder tall enough so that it can be at eye level so that you will not have to look up or down to see it. For this initial session, however, any object will do.

After finding your meditation spot, check to make sure that you have a box, rock or another stationary object to set the focus item on. Try to get it as near to eye level as possible so that the gazing point is situated so that you will not have to put your neck in a strain to look at it.

Mindful Observation Meditation Practice.

☐ After setting up your area, take a moment to get into a comfortable position. You do not want to have to shift your weight or readjust for the time you are in meditation. Remember that the gazing point should be at eye level once you are seated.

☐ Set your intention for the session. Include the amount of time you are going to meditate, and that you are going to effortlessly direct your attention at the object, and that you will allow yourself to see, really see the object differently than normal. Your intention should include that you will observe your body's stillness, and the thoughts that come into your mind for this specified time.

Meditation session steps

☐Set the timer (usually 10 minutes in the beginning)

☐Allow your eyes to rest on the gazing point

- Take a few deep breaths and release the tension from your body
- Allow your body to find that relaxed stillness. Avoid fidgeting by breathing through the impulse
- Think about the size of the object. It's in color. It's texture. Take in the entire presence
- Look at the object as if your seeing it for the first time. Use the eyes of wonder and gaze at it as a child would. What is it? What do you think of it?
- If your eyes wander, gently bring them back. If your thoughts wander, go back to concentrating on the breathing, the back to the object.

How to Finish Meditation

Start to slowly come out of the meditation by stretching and taking a few deep breaths. Since this is an open eye meditation, it would be best to sit for a few moments with your eyes closed. During this time, you can set the intention for the rest of your day, such as "Today is going to be a productive day. I will spend time with my family and friends. I will practice being patient, mindful and have a sense of gratitude for everything and everyone."

Of course, you can have your own intentions, but the main point is not to rush out of the meditation since this can cause stress and tension.

Take another moment to write down your open-eyed awareness meditation. Here are a few suggestions you may consider:

☐ What was your gazing object

☐ What did you notice the most about it

☐ How difficult was it to maintain your gaze on the object

☐ How did this experience compare to other meditation you have tried

How to go deeper into this type of meditation

Meditate on a loved one: you can select a picture of a friend, family member or other loved one. Follow the procedure as above, letting your gazing point be the eyes of the person in the picture. Note in your journal what thoughts you had and/or what memories came forth

Mirror-Gazing Mediation: Sit or stand in front of a mirror and set a timer for 5 to 10 minutes. Follow the same procedure as above. Did you notice anything different about yourself or the thought that comes to mind?

Open-eyed Mindfulness during the day

There is just so much to know about anything and everything. Whenever you think of it during the day, notice something new or different. It may help to state: "There is so much to learn about _____". Don't force it. This should not be a chore or something that causes tension. It is enough to know there is so much to learn about just anything and this will help to open your mind to more and more things.

Chapter 18: Understanding Fear And Anxiety

To better understand stress, it's helpful to bring a better look in the panic response. Anxiety is a normal response to some threat whereas anxiety is unwarranted or inappropriate anxiety. Anxiety and anxiety don't have to be heard. They're unconditioned protective answers. The fear/anxiety answer consists of defensive behaviors, arousal of the adrenal gland and growth in circadian rhythms, and stimulation of the hypothalamic-pituitary-adrenal axis.

Several parts of the brain are involved in fear and anxiety. Neurochemical research and brain imaging methods have enhanced the understanding of this intricate network of interacting structures responsible for these emotions. The cerebral cortex and the amygdala are just two big brain areas involved in the sense of a threat. The cortex is the thinking or cognitive section of the brain. The amygdala is an almond-shaped arrangement that functions as a communications center for the parts of the brain that process incoming sensory signals and interprets the information. It is involved in quick, automatic answers that prepare the brain and body to manage threats and the unexpected. The fear response via the amygdala occurs prior to the bronchial answer and thus the response may be automatic with no person having time to really think about any action. The amygdala can enroll in the presence of risk, trigger a fear response or anxiety and store emotional memories. Various stress symptoms can occur including a heightened startle response, hypervigilance, shortness of breath and facial expression of fear. Greater output from the amygdala is common with all the stress disorders.

The body's reaction to some threat also involves the activation of the hypothalamus which functions as a command center for the hormonal and nervous system of the body. Neurotransmitters are chemical messengers within the brain and hormones carry messages throughout the body. The hypothalamus releases corticotropin-releasing factor (CRF) that activates the release of adrenocorticotropic hormone (ACTH) from the pituitary gland. Adrenocorticotropic hormone stimulates the release of cortisol from the adrenal gland. This stress hormone is released into the bloodstream and has a regulatory effect on the mind, maintaining bodily ethics. Cortisol is involved with complex negative feedback loops. Excessive and continuing secretion of cortisol however can cause adverse health outcomes. The adrenal medulla has direct communication with the brain by way of the sympathetic nervous system. The release of catecholamines prepares a person to the "flight or fight" reaction by inducing such responses as an increased heart rate and blood pressure, a recreation of blood from the inner organs to the muscles, increasing endurance and increasing glucose to offer energy.

The hippocampus is a brain structure that processes traumatic stimuli and helps to encode the data into memories. Associated cues are stored within the hippocampus and these can permit somebody to avoid stimuli that can trigger emotional trauma later on. Studies have revealed that the hippocampus appears to be smaller compared to patients that have endured severe stress like combat or child abuse.

The cognitive charge of anxiety occurs at the lateral frontal cortex that's joined to the amygdala. This allows an individual logically to evaluate a circumstance, modulate influence, control behavioral and interpersonal reactions and regulate autonomic and neuroendocrine function. In the event the stressors are especially difficult, the decreased centers such as the amygdala take over from the executive centers from the prefrontal cortex. When someone suffers from an anxiety disorder, the answer will be restricted to the amygdala-mediated pathways which can be pathological. Different areas of the amygdala may be triggered with the various anxiety disorders and outcomes in different indicators of anxiety. As an instance, people with panic attacks have a fear of dying. Free-floating anxiety is frequent using generalized anxiety disorder. Fear of humiliation is a normal symptom of social anxiety disease. Intrusive obsessions are common with obsessive-compulsive disorder. Emotional memory is more frequent with posttraumatic stress disorder.

There are numerous other brain structures involved in fear and anxiety. These include the cingulate, basal ganglia and striatum.

Life-threatening traumatic experiences can be etched to the amygdala. New favorable memories may decrease more threatening memories but new traumatic experiences or associations can activate original, unfavorable experiences. Anxiety tends to happen with restricted patterns of thinking and behavior and is connected with circuits that are emotionally driven. The panic reaction can be automatic and lifesaving in situations of genuine danger. On the other hand, the stress response as a portion of a learned fear response maybe an overreaction to a comparatively benign situation that could be problematic and may perhaps be disabling. A core problem in anxiety disorders is a faulty link between a stimulus and a response in addition to a misinterpretation of a person's meaning.

What is mindfulness?

People have been practicing mindfulness meditation for millennia. Ancient masters used and taught it for the very same reasons we use it today to become centered, enhance well-being and far better deal with life's inevitable issues. The custom has been revived in our contemporary age especially as a way to manage emotional challenges, chiefly through the work of Jon Kabat-Zinn.

Kabat-Zinn utilizes his Mindfulness-Based Stress Reduction (MBSR) clinic on the Faculty of Massachusetts Medical School Stress Reduction Clinic that he established in 1979. News of the favorable effects of mindfulness on mental and physical wellbeing has spread and mindfulness has become ever well known in the United States as a result.

But what will be Meditation, just? Mindfulness is a type of meditation; however, it's also more compared to meditation. Meditation, as we think of it now, in the Eastern religious tradition that dates back over 5,000 years even predating the Buddhist Tradition that is frequently credited with starting the clinic. Meditation first reached the United States in the 1960s in a secularized form. Meditation is a broad term for the practice of turning inward and becoming still. It includes mindfulness, pilates and much more. Mindfulness comprises this and is also bigger than this. Mindfulness is a way of being with yourself and perceiving the world around you that can help you live your daily life more calmly and with greater equanimity. Jon Kabat Zinn, due to the work of his at the Faculty of Massachusetts Medical School is actually viewed by most as the founding father of the contemporary mindfulness motion.

Chapter 19: Reducing Stress And Anxiety

All the practices outlined thus far in this book have been directed at getting you to understand your mind on a deeper level. Now, it is time to focus specifically on stress and anxiety by introducing a new practice. This new practice will be integrated with everything you have learned so far to form a meditation technique that you can use specifically for releasing stress or anxiety-related issues.

Self-inquiry

The practice of self-inquiry is different from the usual self-help approach. Often, new age spirituality recommends that you dive deep into your beliefs and dissect them with the aim of trying to analyze why you do the things you do. There is some benefit to this, but frankly, given the number of beliefs an average person carries with them, this might not be the most practical way of pursuing self-improvement.

Mindfulness and ancient spiritual practices instead take the view that whether you understand why your beliefs are there or not, the fact is that they exist, and you feel their consequences. So, instead of looking to dissect them, accept them and recognize what needs to change.

Change in this context is not about installing new behaviors but allowing those old beliefs to come up to the surface and express themselves. By not reacting to them negatively and by looking at them equanimously, you weaken the power of these beliefs and this end up deactivating them.

This method actually works extremely well with the way our brain is structured. Our physical brain is a collection of neural networks which store information about our beliefs and all the knowledge we've collected over the years. When a situation arises or a trigger is acknowledged by the mind, the dominant neural network activates, and its supporting networks jump into action as well.

This results in us carrying out certain actions. For example, you've been led to believe over the years the people who cut you off in traffic deserve to be flogged and react negatively every time someone does this to you. Now, imagine if this happens to you and you don't react. You simply recognize that this feeling exists and instead of getting frustrated, you simply go about doing whatever it was you were doing.

Your neural networks operate on a "use it or lose it" approach. If you don't exercise them and act on them, they get weaker and deactivate themselves. Hence, mindfulness and equanimity are really just processes of deactivating these old networks and allowing new behaviors to take their place.

Informal Practice

Let's take a little break from the constant train of formal practices and look at nifty informal practice you can implement self-inquiry with. Remember, an informal practice is something you do as you go about your day, much like the eight pillars of mindfulness. This informal practice will help you become more aware of the presence of some strong, inexplicable emotions.

The truth is that a lot of your stress triggers lie beneath the surface. By triggers, I'm talking about the things that cause you to react to external stimulation. You might not yet be aware of the existence of these triggers and this practice will help you become aware of the existence of them, even if you can't pinpoint exactly what they are.

The first step is to monitor yourself, and whenever you feel a strong emotion, recognize that it is there and accept it. Allow it to be present and don't label it or judge its presence. Counterintuitively, don't even try to dive into why you're feeling like this. Instead, investigate your sensations.

What are you feeling in your body at the moment? Any constrictions or stress? Your breath is a great indicator of this and is often the first thing to react to a stressful situation. Notice if your breath is quickening or has become shallower. This is a clear indication that you're experiencing something stressful. You don't need to panic, but simply acknowledge its existence.

The last step, which is the most crucial, is to recognize that you're able to view this from a third person's perspective. This feeling of stress is happening to you is just one portion of your mind, and you, the one in charge, remains unaffected. Clearly, this means the stress is not about you. Hence, sever your connection with this trigger and keep doing what you were doing.

If the stress remains and you keep detecting it, allow it to remain where it is. All the time, remind yourself that this is not something you identify with. This is tough to practice at first, but with enough repetition you'll see that you'll become better at it.

As a side note: I'm aware of the fact that these practices are all easier said than done. That is the point, after all. Remember, the destination is not what matters. All that you need to focus on is the journey and your experiences along the way. This is how you make progress. If you're able to let go of your stress, even for a split second, that is huge progress.

Exploring Feelings

A huge part of self-inquiry is to turn inwards and face your emotions. This sounds easy to do but we've been trained in our modern world to actively shun them. Perhaps this is because of the fact that facing your emotions is a terrifying thing to do. The fact is that the point of view from which we view emotions is completely flawed.

Think of what it means to describe someone as being "emotional." Being upset is the real implication of that word.

When things go wrong, we become "emotional." When making decisions, we need to be rational and logical. Emotions have gained a bad reputation precisely because we don't know how to handle them, and they spill over when things become unbearable.

Instead of exploring your emotions only during moments of stress, make it a habit to explore them when they arise, or even better, be proactive and go looking for them. You can make this a subset of your sitting practice. During the portion of your practice where you need to acknowledge and allow emotions, spend some additional time exploring them and getting to know them.

So, what does it mean to explore your emotions? There's no logical answer for this, as you can imagine, given the topic on hand. Instead, the best way to describe it is to stay with it and see how it makes you feel. If you feel anger, explore how it manifests in your body and keep taking notes. Do not try to inhibit it or suppress it in any way.

Feel your way forward, and as you stay with your anger, you'll notice that there will be other emotions beneath it. You might think simply realizing a particular feeling exists isn't much help, but you'd be wrong. You see, our brain doesn't remember events just as facts, but also associates emotions with them.

Every memory you have has an associated emotion with it and often you will find that when a similar emotion arises in the present moment, your mind recollects the memory. Emotions are just as valid as the facts you store in your head. So, during your practice, feel your way forward into your emotions.

Let them overwhelm you when you observe them but don't identify with them. Let them simply be and observe them, taking mental notes the entire time. As you observe them, pay attention to how they make you feel physically as well and remain equanimous to the entire experience.

You can do this even during moments of extreme emotion. Find a safe space and close your eyes. Feel the emotion coursing through you. Your mind will probably fly away from the present moment as opposed to wandering but keep redirecting your attention to the swirl of emotions within you and let them consume you. Do not hold them back or consider them invalid.

As you allow them, you'll find that they'll burn themselves out and you'll gain a deeper insight into what is present underneath it and what has really triggered these intense feelings. Usually, some old wound has been touched and this is what is causing you to react out of pain.

This is how you step into your emotions completely. Once you've done this, either as a standalone practice or as part of your sitting meditation, remember to journal your thoughts and experiences in as much detail as you can manage. You'll find that the process of allowing will have dulled the emotions a bit since they'll have spent themselves out. As the emotions drain away, so does your stress.

Inner Rules

I've briefly explored the concept of the "shoulds" before this chapter. These are just your unconscious (and conscious) rules. For the most part, we never react to the world as it is, but rather in terms of what it ought to be. This is against the way the world works due to the fact that a lot of the things that happen to you are outside of your control.

A bigger issue is that your "shoulds" remove you from assessing the situation in the right manner. Here again we see how emotions are misconstrued. By rejecting your emotions as they rise, you store them away and they bubble up at the worst possible moment. This, aligned with your "shoulds," gives you a distorted picture of the world.

A common cause of stress is a lack of recognition in the workplace. How many times have you thought that your boss is a hack and that you're the hardest working person in the office? You feel you deserve a raise and that your boss ought to give it to you thanks to the stellar work you've been producing. Well, have you considered asking them for one?

This sort of thing is a lot more common than you might think. It isn't to do with just raises, but work performance in general. Studies show that employees who speak up and bring their job performance to their bosses' attention receive better pay and experience greater job satisfaction. Ask yourself: Is one of your "shoulds" blocking you from experiencing a better quality of life?

Your inner rules are also what cause great anxiety within you. Every situation you face, you're bringing your assumptions along and this is what colors your experience. So, should you simply let go of all assumptions? Personally, this is a lofty goal to aim for and perhaps impractical.

A better approach would be to simply bring awareness to them and approach things in a checklist-like manner. What I mean is that when you judge something, always ask yourself if you're falling for one of your biases and are distorting reality. A good exercise for you to practice is to journal and reflect on those moments in your life when your assumptions and "shoulds" brought about a negative result for you.

Perhaps you assumed something about someone, and it turned out that you were wrong? Were you emotionally charged and did this distort your view of things? You don't need to dig deep, just jot down those moments. This helps you build a checklist of biases you fall prey to. In addition to this, read up on basic psychological biases that every human being is susceptible to.

There are twenty-five of them, which sounds like a lot, but they are actually easy to understand. I've listed them below:

Incentive caused bias: Rewards for poor decision making.

The halo effect: You love something, so it must be true.

Reverse halo effect: You hate something, so it must be false.

Doubt avoidance tendency: Doubt causing uncertainty, so you rush to judgment.

Confirmation bias: Events confirm what you believe, so you stop looking further.

Curiosity: Can be turned against you. Think about social media "engagement" algorithms.

Golden rule tendency: If it benefits everyone, it must be right.

Envy: Self-explanatory.

Reciprocation: Someone does you a favor/disfavor, so must return it, even if it is a wrong decision.

Narrative fallacy: Associating one thing with another just because it is in close proximity. For example, using pretty women to market household cleaning products.

Pain avoidance: Accepting falsehoods because the truth is painful.

Dunning-Kruger effect: Overvaluing yourself and your possessions. For instance, 90% of drivers estimate they're above average.

Over-optimism: Buying lottery tickets despite the odds always being against you.

Loss aversion: We prefer avoiding pain as opposed to experiencing pleasure.

Herd mentality: Follow everyone else. Everyone says Facebook is great, so you sign up to it. This is the most powerful tendency human beings have.

Contrast effect: Prime yourself for optimism and you'll see everything in that light. Prime yourself negatively and the same event is negative.

Stress influence: We make poor decisions under stress. There is no such thing as high performance under pressure.

Availability heuristic: If it's available, it is used. If it's not present, we ignore it even if it might be relevant.

Use it or lose it: Mentioned above. Exercise your skills or you lose the wiring. Just because you were once great at it doesn't make you an expert still.

Drugs: Substance abuse influences decision making.

Senescence mis-influence: Can't teach an old dog new tricks.

Authority mis-influence: "I was just following orders," said every SS concentration camp guard ever.

Overestimating oneself: Authority in one field doesn't transfer into another.

Reason respective: Combination of number 10 and others. You do things just because you were given a seemingly good reason to do so.

Lollapalooza effect: Small things add up to outsized results, both good and bad. One plus one doesn't equal two in real life.

For more insight into how this list came to be, I suggest reading the highly enjoyable book Poor Charlie's Almanack, which is a collection of the speeches of Charlie Munger, the vice chairman of Berkshire Hathaway Inc.

You don't need to run through this list for every single decision but bring up some of your basic assumptions and beliefs about things and pass them through this list. You'll find that a lot of your beliefs are actually caused by these biases. Not all of them will be true either.

I'd like to point out that giving into these biases doesn't mean you're making a wrong decision. It's just that they are points of manipulation when it comes to your decision making. For example, a lot of social media and advertising exploits every single one of these biases. This doesn't mean the product is bad. It's just that you could be sold a bad product by a skilled manipulator who pushes these buttons well. The aim is to avoid being stupid, as Munger says.

Fighting Biases

Small acts go a long way when it comes to changing your inherent biases and implementing novelty is a great way to do this. Novelty refreshes the brain and gets it curious again. You don't need to go out and overhaul your life but adopting a mindset of constant curiosity (beginner's mindset) is a great way to keep your brain fresh and avoid the mistake of setting things in stone too quickly.

In addition to this, refresh yourself a little everyday by changing your routines just a bit. Drive to work along a different route. Eat somewhere else for lunch or dinner, sleep on the other side of the bed and so on. These acts by themselves won't change your biases, but they will prime you brain to make it more receptive to new information.

Chapter 20: Exercise Your Stress Away

Stress and anger are two of the most unpleasant, difficult to manage emotions that a person could undergo. On the surface, they seem like two entirely different emotions, yet they share certain similarities between them. For one thing, these emotions are present in all of us. Everyone has moments where they've experienced a complete "emotional meltdown" due to stress and anger. We've lashed out at friends, family, co-workers, even perfect strangers at times when either anger or stress got the best of us. It's easy to snap when you feel like you've been pushed to your breaking point and the problem with both anger and stress is, they continue to linger for a long time like a dark cloud that continuously hangs over your head.

Another thing these two emotions have in common is despite the negative association, they can be used for good.

When anger is used for good, it can drive and motivate you to change for the better. For example, when you see an injustice happening, feeling angry about it fuels your desire to make a change for the better. Take marching for women's rights or animal rights for example. Likewise, when stress is used for good, it can be the kick in the butt that you need to take your efforts to the next level. When you've got a looming deadline at work and you've been far too complacent, the stress of finishing in time forces you to double your efforts and deliver what you promised. Small amounts of good stress keep us challenged, motivated, interested, and continuously striving to do better. To be better. Good stress is the adrenaline rush you need to help you overcome the challenges you face so you can cross the finish line of every goal you set for yourself.

When both emotions are bad though, it gets really bad. Anger and stress within a negative context can lead to terrible things like physical abuse, confrontations that escalate into violence and even in the worst-case scenarios, murder. We've heard the stories and news reports about how some people are so blinded by rage they've killed in the heat of the moment. Or done awful things that landed them in jail because they caused grievous harm to another. That is what happens when anger is left unchecked and out of control. Prolonged anger among friends and families can lead to unhappiness, years of not talking to one another and relationships ruined.

The Very Real Problem with Stress and Anger

Without mindfulness, it is going to be hard to release both these emotions from your life. Ever experienced moments where you recalled an argument or a confrontation you had, and the mere thought of it just makes your blood boil all over again? That's what anger can do. It makes you hold onto grudges, makes it hard to forgive, let go and move on. Holding onto that kind of anger is stressful. The problem becomes even worse when you attempt to manage your anger by simply keeping your emotions bottled up inside. Which is what most of us are guilty of. We try our best to suppress that anger, but unfortunately, this is a technique that is very effective long term.

Without mindfulness, it is easy for things to go from bad to worse very, very quickly. When your stress and anger issues are out of control, it begins to poison other aspects of your life. When these emotions are negative, they become toxic, and the absolute worst kind of anger is the kind that results in violent behavior. Especially when it is directed at a loved one or worse, someone who cannot defend themselves against the physical violence you inflict upon them.

Anger, stress, and anxiety are the worst trifecta combination you could have. The three often run so closely together and the emotions become interchangeable that it is sometimes hard to tell where one ends and the other begins. Anger could be triggered by stress, stress could be triggered by anxiety, anxiety could make way for anger which then leads to even more stress. Too much stress in your life could also cause anxiety and anger issues. They run so closely together in fact, that it becomes hard to distinguish stress from the rest at times. Are you feeling stressed? Or has this emotion now crossed over into anxiety? Stress has become a normal part of our everyday living most of us don't even remember what it was like to not feel stressed.

Toxic stress accumulates over time and so does anger. Stress tends to grow and build like a snowball until one day, it bursts forth either in the form of anger or anxiety. This usually happens when you reach a point where you can't take it anymore and everything just feels like it is getting out of hand. Anxiety can sometimes be hard to distinguish from stress, especially if you don't know for sure that you may be dealing with anxiety in the first place. If your worries are more than just temporary, sometimes bordering on fear, and they bother you more often than they should, you could be dealing with more than just stress.You could be dealing with anxiety.

What Kind of Person Do I Want to Be?

Think about the kind of person that you want to be. Obviously, you don't want to be someone who is high strung and stressed out all the time. Nobody wants that. What we all want deep down is happiness at the end of the day. Everything that we do each day is done with the hope that it is going to make us happy. All your choices, decisions, and actions are based on either how this step is going to benefit you or make you happy.

As you begin to ponder and bring awareness to the anger and stress that you feel through mindfulness, spend a couple of minutes thinking about why it was so hard for you to overcome these emotions in the past. Why did you find it so difficult to let go? Can you identify the triggers for your anger and stress? What was the longest you have ever held onto your anger? What coping mechanisms worked in the past? If they didn't work, why?

In the words of Norman Vincent Peele, "If you can change your thoughts, then you can change your will." This is another perfect way to sum up the power of mindfulness.Mind over matter. Your thoughts can move mountains. That is the message mindfulness is trying to teach us.

Exercises for Anger and Stress Management

The road to recovery from anger and stress is going to be a long one. Anger and stress mostly come from within, and to learn how to manage your emotions is going to require a lot of inner strength, discipline, and changing your thought patterns through mindfulness. Only through mindfulness will you be able to change the way that you respond when you feel the anger or stress rising within you.

The best way to begin working on your anger and stress management is to focus on relaxation exercises. One of the many ways that stress manifests itself is through anger, which explains why stressed-out people tend to have a much shorter fuse. They can easily snap at the smallest of things, and everything seems to easily annoy them. Their emotions are at risk of escalating quickly into a full-blown argument or confrontation. Remember that you're trying to exercise change from within, and these exercises are meant to help you manage your stress, and if you're prone to frequent bursts of anger, you're definitely dealing with a lot of stress and tension in your life. It isn't just about calming the mind and finding your inner peace, it is also a method of decreasing the stress levels that are putting pressure on your body, mind, and soul.

High-stress levels daily, anger issues, emotional problems, general feelings of unhappiness all contribute to unhealthy lifestyle habits. Mindfulness and a combination of the right exercises can change all of that. Relaxation exercises are simple, yet just like mindfulness, the benefits that you stand to gain are incredible. Not only do these exercises help you decrease your heart rate and lower your blood pressure, but it can also help to relieve the physical discomfort caused by muscle tension brought on by stress.

Aside from the mindfulness meditation discussed in Chapter 5, here are some other relaxation techniques you can employ to help you better manage your anger and stress levels:

• **Anger Management Exercise #1: Yoga** - A practice like meditation, yoga is a great approach to relaxation whenever you're feeling stressed and angry. Yoga centers mainly around three main principles to help you achieve a state of calm, which are meditation, deep breathing techniques, and controlled physical activity.Its effectiveness lies in its slow, purposeful movements that remind you to be mindful every step of the way. It doesn't put a lot of strain or stress on your body's muscles but instead focuses on building strength through controlled movements. The deep breathing used in yoga teaches your mind and body to relax, opens your muscles and slowly releases the stress from your body with each deep breath in and out that you take. It focuses on balancing, energizing, and awakening your mind, body, and soul. The Asana pose is designed to help your body achieve peace and focus through a series of movements and stretches. Its movements are steady, and comfortable for your body, encouraging you to be relaxed, yet firm during the movement. The movements in this pose will help you greatly reduce your stress and anger levels, and it is something that you should turn to whenever you feel like you might need some calm amidst the chaotic anger in your life.

- **Anger Management Exercise #2 - Hand on Heart Breathing.** Mindful breathing is a useful exercise to have on hand because when faced with anger and tend to lose control of your emotions. Whenever you're under stress and feeling angry, do you notice how your breathing becomes shallow and more tagged? To perform the hand on heart breathing mindfully, start by sitting comfortably in a relaxed position, closing your eyes, and focusing on each breath that you take. Place your hand over your chest where your heart is and continue to breathe deeply in and out, slow, and steady, focus on each inhale and exhale. Focus on the air that is flowing in and out of your body. Breathe in deeply through your nose, and exhale slowly through your mouth. As you breathe in, count to five, pause, relax, and exhale while counting to five again. This repetitive exercise will help you relax, remain calm and learn to be in control of your breathing patterns.

Conclusion

Thank you for taking this journey with me. It would be incomplete had I not included the origins and history of mindfulness and meditation. It is good for you to understand the power of meditation and thus I have included the origins of Buddhist philosophy, which originated from the meditation of Prince Siddhartha Gautama. I have also explained the difference between the different origins as meditation and mindfulness traveled across Asia and practices were adjusted to fit with the beliefs and the customs of the people practicing it. It has now come to the western world and again, there have been changes but none of these change the fundamental fact that meditation consists of being able to breathe in a certain way and using the breath as an anchor for who we find ourselves to be. Although you may not see the relevance at this particular time, I outlined the system that Prince Siddhartha Gautama had made clear to him during his meditation on the fact that mankind was suffering and his attempt to find answers to that suffering. Remember that people from all religions can use Mindfulness Meditation and it won't make any fundamental difference to their religious beliefs other than strengthening them and helping them to experience the foundation of their own individual spirituality. This inner strength and wisdom comes after mindfulness and meditation and has been found by the many practitioners of mindfulness meditation in today's world.

I touched on awareness and as you will have seen in chapter two, gave you several exercises to perform to increase your awareness in different areas of your life. Opening up your senses and your intuitive thought was discussed as well as awareness of self and your awareness of the judgements that you place on the world around you. The problem with judgement is that you limit your responses to life and these tie your hands in responding to difficult situations, whereas dropping judgement helps you to open your heart and to search for solutions as well as finding the kind of empathy that a person needs in order to happily coexist with self and with others. You will see that there are also exercises to open up all of the senses that you were born with including the way you view the world and hear, see, touch and taste life instead of taking things for granted and losing the ability to use those senses to enhance your life. In this world of rush, we are all too quick to ignore what is patently obvious and what lies in front of us because we are too hurried. Mindfulness meditation teaches you the reason why you need to slow down and to enjoy every aspect of life as and when it is offered to you. I also covered the fact that we are inspired by our surroundings and that certain prompts in our lives can help us to remain inspired even on difficult days. That inspiration may come from all kinds of different stimuli but it is a very important part of your life. When you are inspired, you feel enthusiasm to do things. You will know that it is fact that people work better when they work within the parameters of their passions and although this is not always possible, it is possible to use inspiration to gear you up to getting things done and being positive toward your life. The clarity that you gain from meditation also helps in this direction, but certainly not without some form of inspiration to guide you. We have inspiration all around us and while you may be depressed or down with the world, this depression or pulling away from the world can stop you from seeing the bigger picture, whereas mindful meditation takes you back to the roots so that you can be inspired by every little change you find in yourself, your surroundings, in nature or in the way in which you think.

In Chapter three, I spoke about what Mindfulness is and you were given exercises to do that will help you to understand the practice of mindfulness. I would now suggest that you try to purposely incorporate mindfulness into every day of your life, even if this is limited to a small gesture or a kindness toward another human being. A simple smile can convey happiness to strangers, so it is not uncommon that kindness and mindfulness are seen as a very similar type of approach. However, in mindfulness, the moment that matters is now. It's the beginning and it may be the end. Thus the importance of this moment cannot be over-emphasized. This may be the last chance that you get to make an impression in life and thus mindfulness in your actions means that you are living your life with intent and that this intent is deliberately keeping you in that moment until it has gone and has been replaced by another moment. The focus on mindfulness continued into the next chapter, when you were shown how to approach life from a humble stance, how to use nature to inspire you and were presented with exercises that you can do to help you to gain greater control over your mind and the state of your mind at any given time.

Not convinced at this stage?

Well you certainly should have been as the chapters roll out the benefits of meditation and back these up with scientific fact. You will see that the benefits are not limited to the state of mind. In fact, heart health, blood pressure, degenerative diseases and the immune system can all be helped with the use of meditation. It's all set out in plain words so that even a beginner can see a pattern that follows meditation and also understand that what they are doing is well worth the practice, since the overall health benefits have been outlined clearly.

We then talked about the benefits from an individual standpoint, such as how mindfulness meditation improves memory, can help you with pain relief and can even change genetic makeup. You may also find that your practice of meditation helps your posture and that your mobility increases once you are accustomed to and trust the practice of meditation.

The process of meditation was split into different sections so that you learn it correctly and are not sidetracked into starting before you are ready to declare it as part of your lifestyle. I introduced you to breathing methods, different types of approach and breathing exercises that can help you over the course of your working life and even when you are away from home. This chapter assumed that you knew nothing about meditation, but will be useful to even those who have tried and not stuck to it because perhaps the breathing methods used were incorrect or the focus of meditation was misplaced. Many people believe, as I said in the opening, that meditation involves concentration and it's not an unreasonable belief because we are taught all of our lives to concentrate on things that matter. However, as you will have learned, meditation and concentration are two separate entities and the more you try to concentrate, the less likely you are to benefit from the act of mindfulness meditation, which is about being rather than concentrating on being. Staying in the breath and understanding that thoughts will come and go is quite hard for some folk, until they realize the control that they have over those thoughts. Letting go of them and liberating yourself of them when they come at an inappropriate time is as simple as snapping your fingers, once you acknowledge who you are within that moment of meditation. I have given you several tips to try and get rid of the thoughts for the time being. It doesn't mean ignoring them. It simply means letting go of them and enjoying your meditation without letting those thoughts distract you from being in the breath.

The chapter relating to the different types of meditation bears in mind that some people find one type easier to perform than others. There are also types of meditation that you can practice in your everyday life while you are not at home and exercises that help you to make the most of being yourself. The thing that you may struggle with is motivation and this has been covered in this section of the book to remind you to keep yourself inspired although being around inspirational people who make you feel good and reading the right kinds of material can help you in this regard.

Last, but by no means least, I covered the fact that Meditation will change you and the ways in which it will change you.It seemed a fitting end to the book to tell you what to expect from your meditation practice and the changes that you are likely to encounter. These facts were backed up by the experience of a neuroscientist who tried to meditate and who found that unexpected things happened. This impelled her to find out how realistic her teachers were being when they said that she should experience a feeling of wellbeing and kindness toward others, which she first saw as being a slightly "hippy and way out" explanation of what meditation does for you. Her experiments with the mind and the examinations that she subsequently made using people who had meditated and those who had not is convincing and was indeed very convincing to her. It's worthwhile watching her video because she is a down to earth scientist who had all of her questions answered simply by examining mindfulness meditation from a scientific stance and got answers that she was not expecting as well as experiencing for herself the differences that meditation made to her life.

We looked into the workings of the human brain in a last ditch effort to persuade you to continue the practice. This is powerful stuff that cannot be refuted and I thought it appropriate to leave you with that chapter so that you have something to refer to when you experience changes in the way that you think and the way that you react to the world around you.

Thank you for choosing this book and I hope that my words have come over in such a way that you are left with no doubts about how Mindfulness Meditation can change everything you believe and make it so much better. The life that lies ahead of you is an open road. The hurdles that it presents can be dealt with once you have strengthened your mind with mindfulness and meditation. All you need to do now is follow the instructions to the letter and start to begin to appreciate your life and the joy that lies hidden behind all of those thoughts that try so hard to drown out your happiness. Once you let go and start to be in this moment, it will be one of the best moments of your life.

The peace that you seek is not beyond your reach. It has always been there. Your "monkey mind" and your busy lifestyle has stopped you from being able to see it. Once you begin this journey, you will be able to find peace of mind and happiness like you have never experienced before. I wish you well on that journey because I have traveled it myself and am at this moment in time within a moment of breath and clarity that you can also share as your reality. Be in the breath and find out that you really are, appreciating the moments of your life like you never have done in the past. I leave you with a quotation from the original Buddha: